CH

D0761886

ROE v.
WADE

ROE v. WADE

ABORTION AND A WOMAN'S RIGHT TO PRIVACY

by Melissa Higgins

Content Consultant

Joseph W. Dellapenna
Villanova University School of Law

CREDITS

Published by ABDO Publishing Company, PO Box 398166, Minneapolis, MN 55439. Copyright © 2013 by Abdo Consulting Group, Inc. International copyrights reserved in all countries. No part of this book may be reproduced in any form without written permission from the publisher. The Essential Library™ is a trademark and logo of ABDO Publishing Company.

Printed in the United States of America,
North Mankato, Minnesota
042012
092012

Editor: Rebecca Rowell
Series Designer: Emily Love

Library of Congress Cataloging-in-Publication Data

Higgins, Melissa, 1953-
  Roe v. Wade : abortion and a woman's right to privacy / by Melissa Higgins ; content consultant Joseph Dellapenna.
      p. cm. -- (Landmark Supreme Court cases)
  Includes bibliographical references and index.
  ISBN 978-1-61783-476-9
  1. Roe, Jane, 1947---Trials, litigation, etc.--Juvenile literature. 2. Wade, Henry--Trials, litigation, etc.--Juvenile literature. 3. Trials (Abortion)--United States--Juvenile literature. 4. Abortion--Law and legislation--United States--Juvenile literature. 5. Trial and arbitral proceedings I. Dellapenna, Joseph W. II. Title. III. Title: Roe vs. Wade. IV. Title: Roe versus Wade.
  KF228.R59H54 2013
  345.73'0285--dc23

                        2012001275

Photo Credits

Chip Somodevilla/Getty Images, cover, 134; Bettmann/Corbis/AP Images, 1, 35, 37, 41, 45, 55, 77, 94, 108; Bill Janscha/AP Images, 13; Ralf Hettler/iStockphoto, 19; Library of Congress, 27; AP Images, 31, 75, 103; Robert Walsh/iStockphoto, 73; fstockfoto/Shutterstock Images, 91; Barry Thumma/AP Images, 116; lexan/Shutterstock Images, 127; Paul Velgos/iStockphoto, 138

Table of Contents

WHAT IS THE US SUPREME COURT?

The US Supreme Court, located in Washington DC, is the highest court in the United States and authorized to exist by the US Constitution. It consists of a chief justice and eight associate justices nominated by the president of the United States and approved by the US Senate. The justices are appointed to serve for life. A term of the court is from the first Monday in October to the first Monday in October the following year.

Each year, the justices are asked to consider more than 7,000 cases. They vote on which petitions they will grant. Four of the nine justices must vote in favor of granting a petition before a case moves forward. Currently, the justices decide between 100 and 150 cases per term.

The justices generally choose cases that address questions of state or federal laws or other constitutional questions they have not previously ruled on. The Supreme Court cannot simply declare a law unconstitutional; it must wait until someone appeals a lower court's ruling on the law.

HOW DOES THE APPEALS PROCESS WORK?

A case usually begins in a local court. For a case involving a federal law, this is usually a federal district court. For a case involving a state or local law, this is a local trial court.

If a defendant is found guilty in a criminal trial and believes the trial court made an error, that person may appeal the case to a higher court. The defendant, now called an appellant, files a brief that explains the error the trial court allegedly made and asks for the decision to be reversed.

An appellate court, or court of appeals, reviews the records of the lower court but does not look at other evidence or call witnesses. If the appeals court finds no errors were made, the appellant may go one step further and petition the US Supreme Court to review the case. A case ruled on in a state's highest court may be appealed to the US Supreme Court.

A Supreme Court decision is based on a majority vote. Occasionally one or more justices will abstain from a case, however, a majority vote by the remaining justices is still needed to overturn a lower-court ruling. What the US Supreme Court decides is final; there is no other court to which a person can appeal. In addition, these rulings set precedent for future rulings. Unless the circumstances are greatly changed, the Supreme Court makes rulings that are consistent with its past decisions. Only an amendment to the US Constitution can overturn a Supreme Court ruling.

Chapter 1

Looking for Help

On a February afternoon in 1970, 22-year-old Norma McCorvey, a petite woman wearing jeans, sandals, and a shirt tied at her waist, walked into Columbo's, an Italian restaurant in Dallas, Texas. She scanned the red-and-white-checked tables, looking for the two women she had arranged to meet. It did not take long to spot them.

As McCorvey later recalled in her 1994 autobiography, *I Am Roe: My Life, Roe v. Wade, and Freedom of Choice*, the women wore expensive-looking suits that were out of place in the casual restaurant. Linda Coffee was tall, thin, dark, and delicate. Sarah Weddington was shorter, blonde, and slightly plump. They were both a little older than McCorvey, more educated, and more sophisticated.

McCorvey had a ninth-grade education. She had been married and divorced. She drank heavily and did drugs. And, though she was a lesbian, McCorvey was pregnant—the reason for meeting with Coffee and Weddington. Feeling intimidated, McCorvey considered walking away. But she stayed, hoping the pair could—and would—provide what she wanted.

McCorvey shook Weddington's hand and thanked her for coming. McCorvey had little in common with the attorneys—making small talk was uncomfortable. She was eager to get to the point. After ordering pizza and beer, she asked about what she assumed they had come to help her with. McCorvey wanted to know if either of the lawyers knew where she could get an abortion.

When they told her they did not, McCorvey felt angry. Again, she considered leaving. But Weddington, at least, seemed sympathetic to McCorvey's situation, and McCorvey decided to stay. Weddington asked why she wanted an abortion so badly. McCorvey answered that it was hard to find work when she was pregnant. Her mother was raising her first child, whom she hardly ever saw. She was in no shape to be a mother.

Weddington recommended McCorvey not get an abortion. Elective abortions were illegal in Texas, as they were in most other states. Illegal abortions were also dangerous. Every year, women bled to death as the result of abortions, trying to perform them themselves or suffering at the hands of doctors in illegal abortion clinics. Weddington explained that she, Coffee, and a group of other like-minded people were working to overturn the Texas law banning abortion. But they needed a lawsuit to accomplish this and a woman to put her name on the lawsuit—a pregnant woman just like McCorvey.

McCorvey was interested, but she had difficulty keeping track as Weddington described the legal steps the lawsuit would take: district, appeals, state, and federal courts. But she was impressed with Weddington's passion. The two lawyers wanted to hear all about McCorvey. She decided to trust the women and told them her story.

Norma McCorvey

McCorvey was born Norma Leah Nelson on September 22, 1947, in Lettesworth, Louisiana. Her childhood was more unstable than stable.

Her grandmother was a prostitute and fortune-teller. Her mother was an alcoholic and verbally abusive. Her father was a television repairman, though he was not always with the family.

At the age of ten, Norma stole money from a cash register at the gas station where she worked. She wanted to use the money to run away from home. Norma was arrested and sentenced to attend a Catholic boarding school. After misbehaving, she ended up in court again. She was then sentenced to reform school.

During this time, Norma's father left the family. He was gone for a year. When he returned, he moved the family to Dallas. Norma was 15. While working as a server at a drive-in restaurant in Dallas, Norma met Woody McCorvey. He was

> In the 1960s, many women were seeking to expand their boundaries, to be allowed to make choices in their own lives, and to meet the challenges that men had traditionally met in career and life patterns. Women sat in small groups across the country and talked about their role and status and about changing customs and laws they felt were unjust. In Texas, a group of volunteers, primarily women and male ministers, said their state abortion law was wrong. People could sense the imminent possibility of dramatic changes. We thought it was just a matter of time."[1]
>
> —SARAH WEDDINGTON, A QUESTION OF CHOICE

24, handsome, and divorced. They began dating and married shortly after Norma's sixteenth birthday. Soon, Norma suspected she was pregnant and told Woody. Upon hearing the news, Woody beat her. She got a divorce.

Pregnant and lonely, Norma began frequenting gay bars. She had had lots of girlfriends in reform school, and being with lesbians felt comfortable to her. When her daughter, Melissa, was born, Norma hoped her life would improve. But Norma's mother, disgusted by her daughter's sexual lifestyle, took the baby and eventually adopted her after tricking Norma into signing adoption papers.

Though Norma was living with a girlfriend, she began a brief affair with a man she met while working in a Dallas hospital. She became pregnant again. This time, she decided to give up the baby for adoption. After the child's birth, Norma became depressed and drank heavily. She began taking drugs and sometimes sold them.

When an affair with a professional gambler resulted in a third pregnancy, Norma was working in a traveling carnival. She did not want to give up the child for adoption, nor did she feel capable of being a mother. A friend told Norma about abortion. The news was a revelation to Norma; she had not known it was possible.

Though Norma McCorvey, shown here in her thirties, helped change the course of US history, her identity as Jane Roe was kept secret for many years.

Finding a doctor to end her pregnancy became a fervent—and frustrating—quest. Unless the mother's life was at risk, abortion was illegal in Texas. This

MCCORVEY'S RAPE CLAIM

When McCorvey was seeking an abortion, she claimed her pregnancy resulted from rape. She thought the lie would help her situation. The first time she made the claim was to an adoption lawyer she met before McCluskey. He would not help her obtain an abortion. After assuming the child was mixed race, he would not help with an adoption either. McCorvey told Weddington and Coffee the same lie. McCorvey wrote in *I Am Roe*, "The horrible lie—this was the second time I'd used it—pulled at the insides of my stomach."[2] Again, lying did not help. According to McCorvey, Weddington responded, "Well, Norma, it's awful that you were raped. But actually, the Texas abortion law doesn't make any exception for rape. So it doesn't matter in terms of our lawsuit."[3]

requirement made having the procedure difficult, especially for a poor woman with few resources, which Norma was. One referral led her to Henry McCluskey, a soft-spoken adoption lawyer. While she had hoped to get from him the name of someone who could perform an abortion, he instead gave her the name of another attorney: Linda Coffee.

The Best Plaintiff?

After listening to McCorvey's story, Coffee and Weddington asked if she would be interested in being the **plaintiff** in their case. Weddington explained what that meant. McCorvey's involvement would hopefully be minimal. She would probably not have to attend court hearings or answer oral questions. And she would not need to pay anything because Coffee and Weddington would donate their time and money to the case. Also, McCorvey could use a pseudonym to remain anonymous, unless she chose to disclose her identity. McCorvey agreed to be their plaintiff.

After the meeting at the restaurant, Coffee and Weddington considered whether McCorvey was really their best choice for a plaintiff. This would be an important case. If the two young lawyers succeeded in overturning Texas's law, they believed their work would benefit all Texas women. And perhaps they could benefit women in the other 42 states with restrictive provisions for abortion.

Some abortion laws had been changed in recent years to allow for the procedure. In some states, new laws legalized abortion or could be interpreted so broadly that abortion was essentially legal. In time, Coffee and

---

plaintiff—A person or group of people who brings legal action against another person, group, or organization.

Weddington hoped all states might legalize abortion or at least broaden the criteria under which it could be performed. They wanted women to have abortion as an option and for that option to be safe and legal. But in 1970 Texas, as in most other states, abortion **statutes** were still in effect, leaving very few women eligible for legal abortions. Coffee and Weddington were impatient, unsure when abortion reform legislation would pass in their conservative state. They saw the courts as a faster alternative for change.

The lawyers thought their ideal plaintiff needed to meet certain criteria. She would have to hold up under the intense legal and public scrutiny that would certainly result from such a court case—scrutiny that would likely increase for a woman with the kind of history McCorvey had.

Another consideration was McCorvey's desperate desire for an abortion. She was far enough along in her pregnancy that she would have given birth by the time the case concluded. Coffee and Weddington could try to get McCorvey a legal abortion, but it would be a complicated process. It would also be a lengthy one.

statute—A law put into effect by the legislative branch of government.

As a result, McCorvey would be unlikely to get the abortion she desired.

After discussing the pros and cons of McCorvey as their plaintiff, Coffee and Weddington realized the ideal plaintiff simply did not exist. If she were willing to be the plaintiff in the case, the two young lawyers would represent McCorvey in a fight to change Texas's abortion legislation.

The three women met again. McCorvey signed the legal paperwork, setting into motion a case that would become one of the most controversial and divisive Supreme Court decisions in modern US history. ∼

> "I suppose it would be nice to say here that when I made that phone call—after which a woman named Linda Coffee called me back to set up a meeting—I realized I was making abortion-rights history. Or changing my life forever. But the honest truth is that nothing like that even occurred to me. I was simply at the end of my rope. At a dead end. I just didn't know what else to do."[4]
>
> —NORMA MCCORVEY, I AM ROE

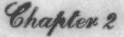

About Abortion

*C*onsidering how often the controversial topic of abortion finds its way into courts, politics, news stories, and religious and moral discussions, one might think it is only a modern issue. This hotly debated topic has been around for as long as abortions have been performed: throughout human history.

Abortion is the termination of a pregnancy and expulsion of an embryo or fetus from a woman's uterus. An embryo is the fertilized egg the first eight weeks after conception, after which it becomes a fetus. Some abortions happen naturally. Miscarriages are natural abortions. The mother's body expels the embryo or fetus before it is viable, likely due to health problems with the mother or the developing baby.

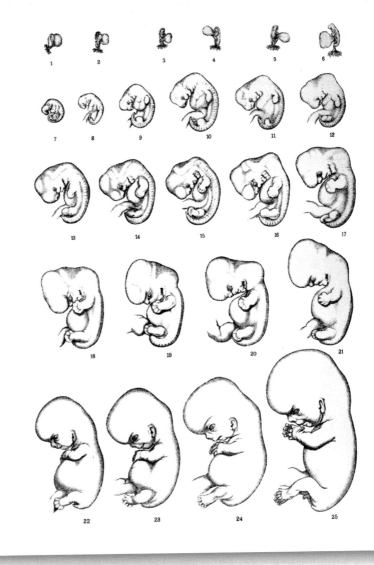

This chart shows the growth of a human
from embryo to 25 weeks.

Abortions can also be caused through artificial
means. Certain herbs and other plants, known as
abortifacients, have been used to expel an embryo or

fetus from a woman's uterus. Today, mechanical methods are more commonly used.

Induced abortions fall into three general categories: elective, eugenic, and therapeutic. In an elective abortion, a woman chooses not to give birth for reasons other than health. A eugenic abortion is performed to prevent the birth of a child with severe birth defects. A therapeutic abortion is meant to prevent serious harm— mental and physical—to the pregnant woman.

The Debate: When Does Life Begin?

At the center of the abortion controversy are very basic questions regarding the beginning of life. People continue to debate whether life begins at the moment of conception, at some point during pregnancy, or at birth. The issue of abortion concerns the status of the embryo or fetus as well and whether it is a human being.

No definitive, universally agreed-upon answers to these questions exist. When life begins is a matter of conjecture and belief. Depending upon one's beliefs, the moral implications are very different. The issue generates many positions. The extreme stances are that a woman choosing abortion is either making a decision that simply affects her own body or one that kills another human being—essentially conspiring with the person performing the abortion to commit murder.

Legal History of Abortion to 1900

Attitudes and beliefs about abortion have varied over time. Abortion has been practiced for thousands of years, though doing so was rare and highly dangerous before 1800. In addition, the legality of abortion was not widely discussed. In some ancient cultures, such as Rome and Greece, abortion was legal if ordered by the child's father—who could also order the death of his wife or his born children—but abortion was not a legal choice for a woman.

ABORTION STANCES

People hold a variety of stances on abortion. There are a range of positions between the extremes of abortion being always wrong and any abortion being acceptable. Some people believe abortion should be allowed only for certain reasons, such as because of rape, incest, fetal deformity, and serious threat to the mother's life or her health—physical or mental. Others think abortion should be allowed only if certain procedures are followed, which may include viewing an ultrasound, listening to a description of fetal life, or obtaining consent from parents, a spouse, or a judge. And yet others feel abortion should be discouraged by providing financial support during and after pregnancy.

EARLY ABORTION RULINGS

Abortion law has been part of US history since colonial times. As such, abortion rulings date back hundreds of years. For example, in *Commonwealth v. Bangs* (1812), the Massachusetts Supreme Judicial Court found Isaiah Bangs innocent of attempted abortion because the prosecution did not successfully prove that the woman was pregnant— that she had quickened. It highlighted the difficulty of proving when a fetus first moves. Seventy years later, in *Commonwealth v. Taylor* (1872), the Massachusetts Supreme Judicial Court held that proving a woman was pregnant was not required to prosecute her abortionist.

Many abortifacients were administered by folk doctors, midwives, and herbalists. Modern medical research has demonstrated that nearly all of these folk remedies were ineffective and the few that might induce an abortion did so by seriously injuring or killing the mother. Infanticide rather than abortion was the common method for disposing of unwanted children before the nineteenth century. The reasons a woman chooses to end a pregnancy were as diverse then as they are today: the inability to afford or care for a child, risk to the mother's mental or physical health, being unwed, or wanting to end a pregnancy due to circumstances such as rape, incest, or an affair.

Early philosophers generally believed an embryo changed from an inanimate part of a woman's body to a separate person some time after conception. Aristotle theorized it was 40 days after conception for males and 80 or 90 days for females. While the Christian church always opposed abortion, between the fourteenth and sixteenth centuries, canon lawyers followed Aristotle's lead and set the moment of ensoulment—when the church believed the developing child was inhabited with a soul—at 40 days for males and 80 days for females. This view gradually shifted, and by the mid-nineteenth century, the Catholic Church deemed abortions at any point in the pregnancy homicide.

In the thirteenth century, the Italian philosopher Thomas Aquinas said that life entered the unborn infant not at a fixed time, but when it first moved inside the mother's womb, about the twentieth week of pregnancy. This state was known as being *quick with child*, which originally meant "alive," and became simply *quickening*. By the nineteenth century, it came to mean "after quickening."

Quickening became the rule of English common law. English legal records from the thirteenth century show that abortions performed as early as the first month of pregnancy were prosecuted as homicide.

> "It is not sufficient that the medical profession should set up a standard of morality for themselves, but the people are to be educated up to it. The profession must become aggressive toward those wrongs and errors which it can only properly expose, and successfully impose."[1]
>
> —*E. P. CHRISTIAN, PHYSICIAN, SPEAKING ABOUT THE NEED FOR EDUCATING PEOPLE ABOUT ABORTION IN 1867*

And in the sixteenth century, abortions were prosecuted as **felonies** in law and church courts and women were prosecuted for aborting their pregnancies themselves. In the seventeenth century, the common law charge for abortion was lowered to a **misdemeanor**. However, if the woman died, it was treated as felony murder.

Early Americans generally accepted the English common law standard. Records show misdemeanor charges were brought against men and women accused of aborting a fetus after quickening. State statutes more explicitly criminalizing abortion began appearing in the

felony—A serious crime, which usually carries a minimum sentence of one or more years in prison.

misdemeanor—A crime belonging to the less serious of the two categories of crime usually carrying a sentence of one year imprisonment or less.

NAPHEYS SPEAKS OUT AGAINST ABORTION

In *The Physical Life of Woman: Advice to the Maiden, Wife, and Mother*, first published in 1870, George H. Napheys shares his opinion about abortion. The physician wrote,

> The detestable crime of abortion is appallingly rife in our day; it is abroad in our land to an extent which would have shocked the dissolute women of pagan Rome.[2]

In the chapter titled "Hints to Young Wives," he wrote about abortion as a crime:

> From the moment of conception a new life commences. . . . The mother who deliberately sets about to destroy this life, either by want of care, or by taking drugs, or using instruments, commits . . . murder, child-murder.[3]

nineteenth century. In 1821, Connecticut became the first state to pass abortion legislation.

Abortion in the United States in the Nineteenth Century

A few reasons have been suggested for why states began passing abortion legislation in the nineteenth century. In 1800, the average American woman had 7 children, compared with 3.5 children by 1900. The decrease in births suggests that people were abstaining from sexual intercourse or using other forms of birth control, of which abortion gradually became one option as the techniques for performing abortions were perfected. The lack of effective contraceptives and disapproval of having a child out of wedlock pressured single women to terminate pregnancies. Prostitution was also on the rise, with an associated increase in abortions. Abortifacients and abortion clinics were highly advertised.

Abortion remained an exceedingly dangerous procedure in the nineteenth century—abortifacients

ABORTION: A COMMERCIAL VENTURE

In the nineteenth century, abortion was big business. Ads in newspapers and women's magazines used veiled language to tout remedies for ending pregnancy. Douches and vinegar sprays would "unblock menses," cold-water baths helped to "remedy sluggish reproductive systems," and electric shocks could "promote menstrual flow."[4] The makers of one patent medicine proclaimed, with a possible hidden message, that their product, "Absolutely must not be taken by pregnant ladies, as it is sure to cause an abortion."[5] Ann Lohman, who operated illegal abortion clinics, is said to have spent $60,000 a year on advertising her clinics and abortion concoctions. Modern research has found that these remedies were completely ineffective or would be effective only by killing the mother. These ads, for the most part, were scams.

These two ads for women were printed in an 1842 New York newspaper. Both mention abortion without using the word abortion. Instead, the ads note *irregularity* and *obstruction*.

were highly toxic, and mechanical techniques were crude. At the same time, American physicians were trying to raise their professional status, having recently formed the American Medical Association (AMA). Many of these physicians lobbied for state abortion statutes. Some researchers conjecture that physicians hoped to end the abortion practices of folk doctors, pharmacists, homeopaths, and midwives to create more business for themselves. Historical evidence also suggests physicians sincerely saw themselves as protectors of the unborn fetus as well as of the mother.

As the physicians' antiabortion campaign became more fervent in the mid- and late-nineteenth century, Protestant churches also took up the cause, with ministers speaking out against abortion from the pulpit. The Roman Catholic Church officially condemned abortion and all birth control in 1869. Pope Pius IX wrote in an official decree that year that abortion was murder at any stage of pregnancy and that the punishment for such an act was excommunication, or a banning from the church. Anthony Comstock, a champion for Victorian moral values, joined the antiabortion crusade in the early 1870s. Prominent newspapers such as the *New York Times* added to public awareness—and outrage—of abortion by running graphic stories of women's deaths at the hands of villainous abortionists.

On the federal level, the US Congress passed the Comstock Act in March 1873, criminalizing the publication, possession, and distribution of devices, materials, or information related to birth control or abortion. It also introduced a number of other morals crimes into federal law. Named for Anthony Comstock, parts of this act would remain in effect as federal law into the 1990s.

Comstock had been made the principle enforcer of the law named after him, and he both arrested and prosecuted violators. In 1878, Comstock arrested a notorious abortion-clinic operator named Ann Lohman.

She committed suicide on the eve of her trial. These events further shifted public sentiment against abortion. Widespread demand for ending the practice emerged. State legislators responded with further antiabortion legislation.

By 1890, every US state had passed abortion legislation. While laws varied by state, most made abortion at any stage of pregnancy a criminal offense, with penalties after quickening more severe, usually **manslaughter**. Most states allowed therapeutic exemptions to save the mother's life. ~

manslaughter—The unlawful killing of someone without meaning to do so.

Chapter 3

The United States, 1900–1970

The increasing antiabortion sentiment and stricter state abortion laws of the late nineteenth and early twentieth centuries was accompanied by a rise in feminism. Under the leadership of women reformers such as Susan B. Anthony, women were seeking the right to vote and more women were attending college and entering the workforce. The concerns of these early feminists focused on domestic improvements, such as better nutrition and sanitation. These early feminists unanimously denounced abortion as "child murder" and as something imposed on women by men.[1] This was especially the case during the early twentieth

Margaret Sanger, founder of the birth control movement, posed in 1916 before leaving a court in New York City, where she was fighting to legalize birth control.

century, when women were encouraged to bear children to help their husbands and country during World War I (1914–1918). Abortions were still performed, but they were secretive acts.

1920s: Birth Control Reform

In the 1920s, Victorian ankle-length skirts gave way to the short skirts of flappers, and a new sexual awakening took place. Times were prosperous and women were returning to the workforce. A "modern" woman could choose whether to marry and how many children to have. In October 1916, Margaret Sanger, a family planning crusader, opened the first birth control clinic in the United States, located in Brooklyn, New York. Although the federal Comstock law banned contraceptives, men and women still obtained them, particularly condoms and diaphragms, which had recently come into use.

By 1938, Sanger and her friends had opened 500 birth control clinics across the United States, and doctors were helping her staff them. The AMA, having by now firmly established itself, saw birth control as good preventive medicine. A majority of physicians wanted the right to counsel their patients and provide them with

> " Infanticide is on the increase to an extent inconceivable. . . . There must be a remedy for such a crying evil as this. But where shall it be found, at least where being, if not in the complete enfranchisement and elevation of woman? Forced maternity, not out of legal marriage but within it, must lie at the bottom of a vast proportion of such revolting outrages against the laws of nature and our common humanity."[2]
>
> —ELIZABETH CADY STANTON, "CHILD MURDER," PUBLISHED IN AN 1868 ISSUE OF THE REVOLUTION, A FEMINIST NEWSPAPER

birth control information. Preventive birth control was also seen as a preferable alternative to abortion.

1930s and 1940s: Abortions Skyrocket

While preventive birth control was preferred, abortions continued. The 1930s and 1940s saw a great change in the procedure. Medical techniques—particularly the advent of antibiotics at the end of the 1930s—made abortion relatively safe for the first time in human history. Another change was in frequency. The number of abortions increased. One cause was the Great Depression of the 1930s, a time during which births declined to the lowest rate in US history. Families experienced great poverty and could afford fewer children. Abortions skyrocketed, with one New Orleans, Louisiana, hospital seeing the number of illegal abortions rise 166 percent in one year, between 1930 and 1931.[6]

In response to the increase in illegal abortions and under pressure by the AMA, Colorado, Maryland, New Mexico, and the District of Columbia passed changes

ABORTION IN THE 1930s

Though the actual number is unknown, physicians have estimated the number of abortions performed in the United States at different times. In his 1936 book, *Abortion— Spontaneous and Induced*, physician Frederick Taussig estimated that 680,000 abortions were performed in the United States in 1935. Other doctors and social scientists have estimated that up to 1 million abortions were performed per year in the 1930s.[7] A study in the late 1940s by Alfred Kinsey found that 24 percent of pregnancies were aborted in 1930, a rate that decreased to 18 percent in 1935.[8] Women of all social classes, races, and religions were represented. Black-market abortion providers included physicians who would perform abortions when their patients requested them, doctors who specialized in abortions, and nonphysicians whose practices ranged from clean and efficient to incompetent rackets. Law enforcement often looked the other way. Careful historical research suggests these numbers were far too high.

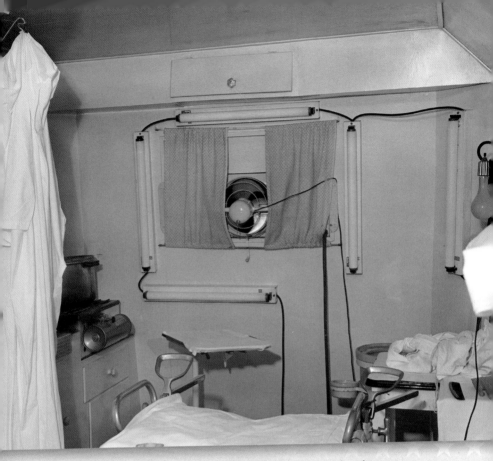

The interior of a trailer used to perform abortions in the 1940s

to their laws that allowed therapeutic abortions to preserve the mother's health. Most other states already permitted physical intervention to save the mother's life, but without clear guidelines for doctors. Only the laws of six states—Florida, Louisiana, Massachusetts, New Hampshire, Pennsylvania, and New Jersey—did not provide an exception for a doctor's discretion.

1950s: Family Values

By the early 1950s, the social climate was changing yet again. The end of World War II (1941–1945) saw the end of the Depression and a growth in prosperity. The nation underwent a conservative shift, with an emphasis on traditional family values and having more children. Parents were married. The mother would stay at home and care for the home and children while the father would work. Women still sought abortions for the same reasons, but the procedure was harder to come by.

Hospital therapeutic abortion committees, rather than individual doctors, were now deciding who was eligible for legal abortions. Many women chose to forgo the difficult and often embarrassing process of obtaining legal abortions, either giving birth or undergoing illegal abortions. A whole industry emerged to place unwanted children—often those born out of wedlock—with adoptive parents. With limited resources, poor women in particular ended up in secret and unreliable abortion clinics.

1960s: The Stage Is Set for Change

By the 1960s, attitudes toward abortion were changing once again. Legal abortions had become relatively

A woman is carried away after the apartment in which she was having an abortion procedure done was raided.

easy and safe. Some doctors were irritated by the rules imposed by abortion therapeutic committees and wanted the opportunity to use their own medical judgment. When two events—an outbreak of rubella and pregnant women's use of the drug thalidomide—resulted in highly publicized fetal deformities, the public became more sympathetic toward eugenic abortions.

From 1960 to 1969, abortion went from being a taboo, rarely talked-about subject to one that was increasingly discussed and debated. This change was the result of several factors. First, the women's movement saw women gaining greater independence. Almost 40 percent of all women worked outside of the home by the late 1960s, and careers were being extolled over motherhood.[9] Next, similar to the feminism of the 1920s—and due partly to wide use of the new birth control pill—there was a more relaxed attitude toward sex. Marriage and children were becoming choices for women rather than requirements. Also, with high unemployment and inflation, couples were often waiting longer to have children. Finally, a general concern about worldwide population growth added to a more favorable attitude of some people toward methods that would control reproduction. Women were gaining in the choices they could make about their lives and their bodies. These options included not having or postponing having children, which meant preventing or ending pregnancy.

The social and political climate was favorable for legal reform. Between 1967 and 1970, 13 states changed their abortion laws, adopting all or parts of the American Law Institute's 1962 *Model Penal Code*. It proposed that physicians should be allowed to terminate a pregnancy

THALIDOMIDE BABIES

In 1962, Sherri Finkbine, the host of the popular children's television program *Romper Room*, was living in Arizona with her husband and four children. While pregnant with her fifth child, she read stories of babies in Europe being born deformed as a result of their mothers taking a tranquilizer called thalidomide—a drug Finkbine had been taking. Realizing there was a high probability her baby would be born deformed, she tried to get certification from a hospital therapeutic committee for a legal abortion.

Because Arizona, like many states, allowed abortions only to save the mother's life, Finkbine stretched the truth, claiming the birth would cause her grave harm. While these arguments were standard practice and the requests usually approved, Finkbine's request took a lengthy legal course, and she ended up getting an abortion in Sweden. The fetus was badly deformed. The highly publicized drama helped sway public opinion.

if they believed "(1) that continuation of the pregnancy would gravely impair the physical and mental health of the mother or (2) that the child would be born with grave physical or mental defect, or (3) that the pregnancy resulted from rape, incest, or other felonious intercourse."[10]

In 1969, the California Supreme Court ruled in the case *California v. Belous* that the California abortion law was too vague with regard to preserving the woman's life. Subsequent legislation allowed abortion to protect the health of the woman, which doctors interpreted to include mental health. This made abortion virtually legal in California. Hawaii, Alaska, New York, and Washington legislatively removed all restrictions on the reasons abortions could be performed early in pregnancy, with New York's 1970 law being the broadest: all abortions were permitted within the first 24 weeks of pregnancy, there was no residency requirement, and hospitalization was not required unless it was after the twelfth week. Should the procedure take place after the twentieth week, a second doctor was required to be present to handle medical care of any live birth. For the most part, these changes were pressed by male doctors and attorneys. Women did not become prominent in the abortion reform movement until 1969.

Cultural changes during the 1960s prompted many women to pursue issues important to them, including abortion.

Legislative change stopped in 1970. Several states rejected proposed changes. In addition, New York's legislature voted to repeal its 1970 law, but the governor issued a veto, which kept the law in place. Complete repeal of all state laws would come about only if new federal legislation passed or if a case decided by the US Supreme Court settled the matter. By 1970, court cases challenging state abortion laws were cropping up across the country. One such case was about to be filed in Texas. ~

Chapter 4

Two Young Attorneys, One Historical Moment

During the 1960s, women were gaining greater independence while still under the influence of 1950s traditional values. Coffee and Weddington were among 40 women attending the University of Texas Law School in 1965, but they were the only two women in their graduating class who did not postpone practicing law until after they married and had children.

Like many young women at the time, Weddington had to overcome society's long-held ideas about females being inferior to males. When her college dean advised her not to attend law school because it would be too strenuous for her, Weddington decided she would go. And on another occasion, when a banker told Weddington, who was married, her husband would have to cosign her application for a credit card, even though she was supporting herself as an attorney, Weddington refused to apply.

It was in 1968, after hearing women's stories of injustices similar to her own that Weddington began thinking about how she could effect change. Weddington heard stories of women who had died or were severely injured as a result of going to illegal abortion mills or trying to self-induce abortion using dangerous drugs, fluids, or mechanical means. Because abortion was legal in Texas only to save a pregnant woman's life, young, poor, and less sophisticated women typically did not have the means to find safe and legal abortions. Having had an abortion herself, Weddington was especially sympathetic to these women's experiences. Legalizing abortion would allow women greater control over their bodies. It would also make abortion safer. Weddington began volunteering for an abortion referral group doing legal research.

The Seeds of a Case

In 1969, the home Weddington shared with her husband, Ron, became the base for fund-raising activities for causes Weddington actively supported. During one yard sale, a volunteer from the abortion referral group shared with Weddington that, due to worry over being arrested, the group was having to decrease its visibility and was not reaching the women who needed them. Weddington noted,

> A high school physical education instructor told us, 'Young women must preserve their reproductive capacity; after all, it is their meal ticket.' I took a silent vow that I would have a meal ticket other than reproductive capacity."[2]
>
> —SARAH WEDDINGTON, A QUESTION OF CHOICE

> To serve more women, the project needed to be more public; yet some volunteers worried about the personal ramifications of changing the way they operated. They wondered whether the authorities would continue to leave them alone if they moved into the spotlight.[1]

Because abortion was illegal in most instances, publicity would bring attention to the group—

Sarah Weddington was the lead attorney on the *Roe* case. Her determination to change Texas's abortion law changed the United States.

attention to their work that supported illegal behavior. That focus could do more harm than good. Arrests could further limit the referral group from helping those women who wanted or needed an abortion.

Finding a solution to the referral group's problem sent Weddington to research the Texas abortion statute. Originally passed in 1854, the Texas law made it illegal to perform an abortion. The two- to five-year penalty

WEDDINGTON'S ABORTION EXPERIENCE

Weddington found herself in the same situation as many young women in the 1960s—pregnant and seeking an illegal abortion. It was not unusual for women with money to travel to countries where abortion was legal. But as a struggling college student, Weddington did not have such resources. She did, however, learn of a foreign abortion clinic she could afford—using her entire savings of $400— across the Texas border in Mexico.

While abortions were illegal in Mexico, women were rarely arrested. Weddington traveled to the clinic and was relieved to find a clean facility with professional staff. She recalled the experience in her book, *A Question of Choice*:

Now I know there were countless others living out their own private scenes when abortion was illegal. Some of them were not as lucky as I; they ended up in awful places, they were operated on by people with no medical skills.[4]

doubled if the woman did not consent to the procedure. Any death related to an abortion was defined as murder, and anyone supplying abortifacients or helping a woman get an abortion could be charged as an **accomplice**.

The only exception to the law was for an abortion by "medical advice for the purpose of saving the life of" the mother.[3] But as with other similarly written state statutes, doctors in Texas were unsure how to interpret which situations warranted saving the life of the mother. Many physicians avoided potential criminal charges by not performing abortions at all. The Texas law was restrictive compared with those of some other states; it had no provisions for abortion in cases of rape, incest, fetal deformity, or health of the woman.

As Weddington expanded her research into the history of abortion, she read US Supreme Court cases. One case in particular caught her attention: *Griswold v. Connecticut* (1965). It made an argument for personal privacy—an argument she thought could relate to women seeking abortions.

Griswold v. Connecticut (1965)

Unlike abortion, preventive birth control gained public acceptance during the first half of the twentieth century. By the early 1960s, birth control devices were legal in every state except Connecticut. The Planned Parenthood League of Connecticut (PPLC) had been fighting since the 1930s to change its state's law banning birth control. The organization came upon stiff opposition from the

accomplice—Someone associated with a person who has committed a wrongdoing.

Catholic Church and legislators who believed the ban was good for public morals and worried the law's repeal would be the next step toward legalizing abortion.

Frustrated with the lack of movement in the Connecticut legislature, the PPLC sought a court ruling, arguing that the state's ban on birth control violated the Fourteenth Amendment's **due process** guarantee of life and liberty. Its efforts were blocked in the Connecticut courts, but one case, *Griswold v. Connecticut* (1965), finally made its way to the Supreme Court. In the landmark decision on this case, the court ruled that the law banning the use of birth control violated an inherent right of privacy found in the US Constitution. In this case, it was the right to marital privacy.

Justice William Douglas wrote the **majority opinion** in the case. In it, he refers to the marital relationship:

> *The present case, then, concerns a relationship lying within the zone of privacy created by several fundamental constitutional guarantees. And it concerns a law which, in forbidding the use of contraceptives . . . seeks to achieve its goals by means having a maximum destructive impact upon that relationship. Such a law cannot stand in light of the familiar principle, so often applied by*

this Court, that a "governmental purpose to control or prevent activities constitutionally subject to state regulation may not be achieved by means which sweep unnecessarily broadly and thereby invade the area of protected freedoms."[5]

In other words, Connecticut law violated rights set forth in the US Constitution—rights the court regularly rules on. Using contraception is a married couple's right. And because the law in question applied to single and married people alike, it was deemed **unconstitutional**. The justices holding the majority ruling did not agree which amendments specifically applied to the case, but they did agree to a couple's right to privacy.

A Request to File a Texas Case

Although she wasn't finding an answer to the abortion referral group's problem, Weddington felt encouraged by the *Griswold* case and by the court cases and

due process—As provided by the Fifth Amendment to the US Constitution, the promise that the government will follow the law and fair procedures when interacting with the people.

justice—A member of the US Supreme Court.

majority opinion—An explanation of the reasoning behind the majority decision of the Supreme Court.

unconstitutional—Inconsistent with a constitution.

FEDERAL COURT

The judicial branch of the federal government was established under the US Constitution along with the legislative and executive branches. It includes federal courts, which were defined by the US Congress per the Constitution. The federal court system has 94 US district courts organized into 12 regional circuits, each with its own court of appeals. If a party in a lawsuit is unhappy with the decision made by the US district court ruling on the case, that party may appeal to the US court of appeals in that circuit. If still unsatisfied, the party may ask the US Supreme Court—the highest court in the nation—to review the case. It hears cases that deal with the constitutionality of laws, as in *Roe v. Wade*, and areas of law that arise in cases involving federal law issues such as disputes between two or more states, bankruptcies, and treaties.

legislation cropping up across the country challenging or changing state abortion laws. One day in 1969, two of Weddington's friends asked if she would file a lawsuit challenging the **constitutionality** of the Texas abortion statute in federal court and add their case to others being filed on the federal level. Their hope was that one of these cases would be heard by the Supreme Court.

Weddington had graduated from the University of Texas Law School only in 1967 and had never handled a contested case. Still, her friends respected the research she had already done and believed the case should have a female lawyer since it was a women's issue. Plus, Weddington was the only attorney they knew who might be willing to do the work for free. Although afraid of failing and uncertain she was really the right person for the job, Weddington agreed.

Finding Plaintiffs

Weddington began gathering a group of people to assist her with the case, including Coffee, her law school classmate. Coffee was living in Dallas at the time and working as an attorney in a bankruptcy firm. She had **clerked** for a federal judge, and Weddington was eager for Coffee's federal court expertise.

In December 1969, Coffee readily agreed to help, and the two attorneys began meeting to discuss strategy. They needed one or more plaintiffs "who could show a personal, direct, significant impact of the Texas anti-abortion statutes," Weddington remembered.[6] It would become an ongoing worry as they drafted the complaint and lined up their legal points.

---

clerk—To work for a judge and assist with records, research, and other legal matters as needed.

constitutionality—Being in accordance with a constitution.

DEATHS DUE TO ILLEGAL ABORTIONS

The number of women who died in the 1960s as a result of illegal and self-induced abortions is difficult to determine. Illegal abortion doctors did not report deaths for fear of criminal prosecution, and physicians who treated women for abortion-related injuries often altered their records to avoid embarrassment for their patients. While some estimates place the number of abortion-related deaths as high as 8,000 to 10,000 per year in the 1960s, other estimates are much lower, at 1,000 to as few as 100 per year.[7] The low numbers may be because the use of abortifacients—the most dangerous method of abortion—was not common in the 1960s. In addition, illegal abortions were usually performed by trained physicians using current surgical techniques, which made the procedure safer for the women having it done.

The lawyers' first selection as plaintiff was a woman who was not pregnant, but, due to a neurochemical disorder, was advised by her doctor to avoid getting pregnant and not to take birth control pills. If the contraception method the woman and her husband used failed and she became pregnant, her health would be at risk without an abortion. An abortion under these conditions was illegal in Texas. The couple wanted to be plaintiffs because they believed the Texas law compromised their right to normal marital intimacy. They would become "John Doe" and "Mary Doe."

Weddington and Coffee needed an additional plaintiff, a pregnant woman who wanted an abortion. A friend of Coffee's, attorney Henry McCluskey, called her with a referral—a young, pregnant woman living in Dallas who was looking for an abortion. Coffee talked to the woman and arranged for Weddington to meet them at an Italian restaurant in Dallas. The pregnant woman's name was Norma McCorvey. She would become "Jane Roe." Their plaintiffs selected, Weddington and Coffee now had to construct and file their case. ~

> We still had to name our plaintiffs. We picked names that rhymed. I liked 'Jane Roe.' To me the name represented all women, not just one. We decided on 'John and Mary Doe' for the couple. The names seemed generic."[8]
>
> —*SARAH WEDDINGTON, A QUESTION OF CHOICE*

Chapter 5

Constructing and Filing *Roe v. Wade*

Weddington and Coffee decided to file two separate lawsuits to challenge Texas's abortion statutes. They did that because the issues in each case were slightly different: one of their plaintiffs was pregnant and the other was not. Filing two cases would also increase their chances of at least one case landing in the court of Judge Sarah Hughes. As Coffee's former boss, Hughes would probably be sympathetic to their cause. Once one case was assigned, Coffee and Weddington planned to request the other case be joined with it so they could present a single case with combined facts.

Estelle Griswold, *left*, and Cornelia Dickerman Jahncke respond to the favorable ruling in the *Griswold* case. The case encouraged Weddington in her efforts to legalize abortion in Texas.

The women also requested that a federal three-judge court hear their case, since a state court could not determine their constitutional rights. The lawyers strategized that because a three-judge court included one member of the circuit court and two judges from district court, its decision would carry more weight than that of a single-judge federal court. In addition, three-judge courts were required to proceed with cases as quickly as possible, which meant Coffee and Weddington—and their pregnant plaintiff—would get a speedy hearing.

Unlike many legal documents, the filing documents Coffee drafted in February 1970 were not lengthy: only three legal-sized pages. In the petition, the lawyers asked the court to do two things. First, they wanted

THREE-JUDGE COURTS

The federal court system has three levels: district courts, courts of appeals, and the Supreme Court. Federal three-judge courts are the intermediate level—courts of appeals. They are composed of one circuit judge and two federal district judges. Three-judge courts were established in 1910 to provide a greater check on the powers of federal one-judge courts.

In 1937, an additional act required a three-judge court to hear cases where the constitutionality of a state law was challenged. Because safeguards were soon put in place to eliminate the power issues of single-judge courts, three-judge courts were rarely used. Then, in the 1960s, civil rights attorneys discovered they were an effective way to take cases directly to the Supreme Court, as the system sometimes allowed lawsuits to bypass federal appellate courts, courts that can review the judgment of another court.

the court to affirm that the Texas abortion statutes were unconstitutional. Second, they wanted the court to order a stop to enforcement of those statutes. Weddington recalled,

> *In essence, we wanted the court to say the Texas anti-abortion laws violated the US Constitution and to tell local law enforcement officials to quit **prosecuting** doctors under those statutes.*[1]

Their argument also consisted of two points. First, the Texas law violated an individual right of privacy secured in the Constitution's First, Fourth, Fifth, Eighth, Ninth, and Fourteenth amendments. Second, the Texas statutes were too vague for doctors to understand and act upon.

In the documents for Jane Roe's case, Coffee also included a seven-point statement of facts. Facts one through five were specific to McCorvey's situation. They stated that Roe was an unmarried pregnant woman who, due to economic hardship and the social stigma of having an illegitimate child, wanted to end her pregnancy with an abortion performed by a licensed physician in safe circumstances. Because her life was not

---

prosecuting—Bringing legal action against someone.

threatened by her pregnancy, she could not secure a legal abortion under Texas law and did not have the funds to travel to a location outside of the state where she could obtain a safe abortion.

Facts six and seven were more general:

6. *An abortion performed by a competent, licensed physician under hospital or clinic conditions is a safe and simple procedure which presents less danger to the pregnant woman than ordinary childbirth.*

7. *An abortion performed outside of the clinical setting by unqualified personnel is extremely dangerous and often results in death, maiming, sterility, or serious infection.*[2]

On the evening of March 2, 1970, Coffee and Weddington made a few final changes to the documents. The following day, March 3, Coffee walked to the federal courthouse in Dallas, paying $30 of her own money to file the two cases. Roe's case was **docketed** as case number 3-3690-B. By naming as their **defendant** the highest-ranking official responsible for law enforcement in Dallas County, Texas—District Attorney Henry Wade—the case took on the title *Roe v. Wade.*

OPPOSITION TO ABORTION AT THE TIME OF *ROE V. WADE*

During the 1960s, people opposed to abortion generally stayed on the sidelines, not believing that abortion-on-demand could ever become a reality. But in the late 1960s and early 1970s, with the rise of state abortion-reform legislation, a new right-to-life movement mobilized. Organizations such as the National Right to Life Committee and the Voice of the Unborn formed, actively fighting state legislation and targeting pro-choice political candidates. The Catholic Church and others also actively lobbied legislators and rounded up support among its members to oppose abortion reform.

Henry Wade

Wade was already famous for prosecuting Jack Ruby, the murderer of Lee Harvey Oswald, John F. Kennedy's assassin. Wade was known as a tough **prosecutor**—he would send 29 people to **death row** during his career. The son of a judge, Wade grew up near Dallas and

death row—The part of a prison where prisoners who have been sentenced to death for their crimes live until they are killed.

defendant—The person against whom legal action is brought.

docket—To put on a court calendar.

prosecutor—A lawyer who brings legal action against someone.

graduated with highest honors from the University of Texas. He was not a proponent of feminist causes, but he also did not actively prosecute abortion cases, bringing few to trial. In 1970, Wade did not seem especially aware that abortion laws were under attack across the country or that abortion unrest was brewing in his state.

As a district attorney, Wade had a team of attorneys to whom he could give cases. He chose not to represent himself. Rather, Wade assigned *Roe* and *Doe* to Assistant District Attorney John Tolle, who handled federal cases.

Judges and Court Date Determined

The chief judge of the **US Court of Appeals** for the Fifth Circuit, John R. Brown, named the judges in the three-judge panel. As Coffee and Weddington had hoped, one of their cases landed in the court of Hughes. She was joined by William M. Taylor and Irving L. Goldberg. Taylor was a federal district judge, and Goldberg was a federal circuit judge.

It was agreed that the *Roe* and *Doe* cases would be combined. They would be referred to simply as *Roe*. The trial was set for May 22, 1970.

THE FIFTH CIRCUIT

The federal courts of appeals are divided into 12 circuits by geographic area. The word *circuit* comes from when judges rode the circuit via transportation such as horse and stagecoach to hear cases across their territory. When *Roe* was heard in the US Court of Appeals for the Fifth Circuit, the circuit included Alabama, Florida, Georgia, Louisiana, Mississippi, and Texas. It was especially known for its ruling in *Bell v. Rippy* (1961), which upheld *Brown v. Board of Education* (1954) and required Dallas to integrate its public schools.

Additions to the Case: A Plaintiff and a Class Action

On March 19, two Dallas attorneys—Fred Bruner and Roy L. Merrill Jr.—asked to have a third plaintiff added to the *Roe* case. The attorneys' client, James Hallford, was a doctor who had performed abortions for years and had been **indicted** under the Texas abortion law for performing an illegal abortion. Bruner and Merrill argued that the state statute was so vague and difficult

---

indict—To officially decide that someone should be put on trial for a crime.

US Court of Appeals—A federal court that hears cases appealed from the district courts in its circuit.

MCCORVEY'S RAPE CLAIM: WEDDINGTON'S VERSION

Weddington wrote in her own book, *A Question of Choice*, that McCorvey "asked if it would help if she had been raped."[3] Weddington went on to explain that she asked about witnesses, a police report, any proof of rape, and that McCorvey said there were not. Weddington wrote,

> *Neither Linda nor I questioned her further about how she had gotten pregnant. I was not going to allege something in the complaint that I could not back up with proof. Also, we did not want the Texas law changed only to allow abortion in cases of rape. We wanted a decision that abortion was covered by the right of privacy. After all, the women coming to the referral project were there as a result of a wide variety of circumstances. Our principles were not based on how conception occurred.*[4]

to interpret that Hallford could not determine when a woman's life was in danger. Weddington and Coffee were glad to add the physician's case to theirs, believing it made *Roe* stronger. The request was granted.

Coffee and Weddington had always imagined their case affecting more than McCorvey, their Jane Roe, including the many women facing unwanted pregnancies. The two young lawyers considered the case a good candidate for a **class action**. The women also considered a class action a good choice because their plaintiff would not be pregnant much longer. After McCorvey had her baby, the state could argue that the case was no longer meaningful. By making *Roe* a class action, Coffee and Weddington could counter that argument by saying somewhere in Texas a woman was pregnant and desired an abortion. But they had not had time to pursue a class action due to McCorvey's pregnancy and their haste to file the case. After filing *Roe*, Coffee and Weddington began researching the requirements of a class action suit. They amended their case prior to the May 22 court date.

The Lawyers Prepare

In the two months preceding the hearing, Coffee and Weddington filed **affidavits** and a **brief** outlining their positions, primarily that a right to privacy was protected by a combination of provisions under the Constitution. In this case, the right to privacy was a woman's right

affidavit—A statement made under oath, witnessed by an individual with legal authority.

brief—A document that establishes the legal arguments of a case.

class action—A lawsuit filed on behalf of every person in that situation.

to control her body. Coffee and Weddington included citations of cases that supported their arguments, including the Supreme Court's majority opinion on the birth control case, *Griswold v. Connecticut* (1965), and the inherent guarantee in the Constitution for the "zones of privacy" noted in the ruling.[5] The two lawyers additionally mentioned the concepts of privacy found in the Ninth Amendment, as discussed in *Griswold*, and the rights and liberties determined to be in the Fourteenth Amendment in other cases.

Tolle represented Wade and the Dallas County District Attorney's Office. He was a World War II

THE NINTH AMENDMENT

The original ten amendments to the Constitution, known as the Bill of Rights, were passed by Congress in 1789 and ratified in 1791. Since then, 17 amendments have been added, for a total of 27 amendments. The Ninth Amendment figured prominently in the *Roe v. Wade* case. It states, "The enumeration in the Constitution, of certain rights, shall not be construed to deny or disparage others retained by the people."[6] The amendment was included because some rights were defined and not all rights could be. In essence, the amendment covers those rights not specifically addressed elsewhere in the Constitution, meaning that lack of specific mention does not mean the right is not covered.

veteran, a low-key and accomplished prosecutor, and a Roman Catholic. Tolle based his objection to *Roe* on the principle that life begins at the time of conception and, therefore, the state was obligated to protect that life. Tolle believed so strongly in this argument that he did not address Weddington and Coffee's right-of-privacy line of reasoning, assuming that if a fetus were a human being separate from its mother, the mother then had no right to control it. In other words, the mother's right to privacy was doubtful. Tolle also argued that because the Texas abortion law affected only the person who performed the abortion and not the woman who had the abortion, Jane Roe did not have legal standing—the law did not apply to her. Tolle filed his objection with the court on March 23. The three lawyers would soon argue their cases in district court and learn if the judges agreed with their strategies. ∼

Chapter 6

The Dallas Hearing

The trial of *Roe v. Wade* began May 22, 1970, in the Dallas federal courthouse before Judges Hughes, Goldberg, and Taylor. Weddington worried she and Coffee might be met at the court by antiabortion demonstrators, but the few demonstrators present were abortion supporters. Members of the press and mostly women packed the courtroom. Since McCorvey was far along in her pregnancy, she did not attend. Coffee and Weddington were ready to give their **oral arguments**. If they were nervous, it was understandable. Coffee had not handled a case this large, and Weddington had never argued a contested case or appeared before a federal judge.

Arguing for Abortion

Coffee spoke first. According to some observers, she looked disheveled, as if she had not combed her hair. Coffee covered the technical aspects of the *Roe* argument. She explained why the federal courts should hear a case involving state law. She emphasized that the plaintiff's goal of getting an abortion could be met only with an **injunction** against the prosecution of abortion doctors. Because federal courts are mandated by Congress to defer to state laws whenever possible, the judges asked Coffee why she did not simply go through the Texas legislature and courts to broaden the state's law to include more medical exceptions for abortion. In response, Coffee listed the reasons why the Texas law was unconstitutional based on fundamental protections guaranteed in the First, Fourth, Fifth, Eighth, Ninth, and Fourteenth Amendments. Her goal was to persuade the judges that Roe had a constitutional right to control her body.

The judges seemed uninterested as she discussed the First Amendment and a doctor's right to freely associate

injunction—A court order commanding or forbidding something.

oral argument—A spoken presentation of a legal case by a lawyer.

with his or her patients. Goldberg asked about the Ninth Amendment, wondering if it could serve as a basis for a sweeping right to reproductive privacy, as it had in *Griswold v. Connecticut* (1965). Coffee agreed but added,

> *I don't think it makes any difference . . . whether you say that the rights involved are First Amendment rights or Ninth Amendment rights; I feel they are so important that they deserve the special protection that has been accorded to First Amendment rights.*[1]

After making a few more points, Coffee finished her oral argument. It was then Weddington's turn to speak.

Weddington was nervous and lacked confidence, but she appeared calm and sounded self-assured to

THE FOURTEENTH AMENDMENT

The Fourteenth Amendment was a focus of the *Roe v. Wade* case. Section 1 of the Fourteenth Amendment, known as the due process clause, states,

> No state shall make or enforce any law which shall abridge the privileges or immunities of citizens of the United States; nor shall any state deprive any person of life, liberty, or property, without due process of law; nor deny to any person within its jurisdiction the equal protection of the laws.[4]

Weddington and Coffee asserted in *Roe v. Wade* that the Fourteenth Amendment right to liberty was being violated. They argued that a woman seeking an abortion was not being granted her right to privacy, which included her right to end her pregnancy.

others. She told the three judges that life was an "ongoing process" and that it was almost impossible to pinpoint exactly when life began.[3] She had planned on citing court cases in which the fetus did not have the legal rights of a person but was interrupted by Goldberg. He asked if Weddington could imagine the state having any justification for regulating abortion, such as if the woman was married or not, or if the procedure was performed in a hospital or a doctor's office. Weddington did not see any compelling state interest. After a few more questions and responses, her time came to an end. Next, lawyers representing Wade would speak.

Arguing Against Abortion

Although Wade's office, a county department, was responsible for much of the initial preparation for the case, the state attorney general's office took over the case. Robert Flowers, head of the enforcement division under which *Roe v. Wade* fell, assigned the case to Jay Floyd, his assistant chief.

Just as Tolle had done in his written objection to *Roe v. Wade*, Floyd based his defense of the Texas abortion law on life beginning at conception—that destroying an infant in the womb is murder. But Floyd opened his argument to the judges by saying the case should be dismissed because there was no real controversy. Texas law did not punish women for having an abortion, and Roe had already given birth or must have been so far along in her pregnancy that she could not have an abortion. After a cool reception from the judges on this point, Floyd moved on to say that a right to abortion could not be found anywhere in the Constitution, particularly not in the First Amendment.

When asked by Goldberg about possible protections in the Ninth Amendment, Floyd did not address this question directly. Instead, he argued that the state had an interest to protect the fetus. When asked by the judges if an abortion would be acceptable if a woman were at risk of imminent death, Floyd declined to make what he said was a medical judgment.

> "If any person shall designedly administer to a pregnant woman or knowingly procure to be administered with her consent any drug or medicine, or shall use towards her any violence or means whatever externally or internally applied, and thereby procure an abortion, he shall be confined in the penitentiary not less than two nor more than five years; if it be done without her consent, the punishment shall be doubled. By 'abortion' is meant that the life of the fetus or embryo shall be destroyed in the woman's womb or that a premature birth thereof be caused."[6]
>
> —*ARTICLE 1191. ABORTION, TEXAS PENAL CODE, WHICH* ROE V. WADE *WAS FIGHTING*

Tolle then took the floor. He addressed the state's right in making these decisions, saying the state had "a right to protect life . . . in whatever stage it may be in . . . and if there is no absolute fact as to when life occurs, then it becomes . . . a legislative problem as to when [the legislators] are going to set up an arbitrary time."[5]

He added that a child's life was more important than a woman's right to privacy. After Tolle's remarks, the hearing ended.

The Decision

Even with her friends' assurances that the hearing went well and the state's case was not as strong, Weddington was unhappy with her performance in court. She and Coffee eagerly—and anxiously—awaited the court's decision. It came more than three weeks later.

On June 17, 1970, in a unanimous decision, the three-judge court declared the Texas abortion law unconstitutional and determined that Roe and Hallford, the physician also named in the case, were appropriate plaintiffs. However, the judges found that John and Mary Doe did not show an actual case because the wife was not pregnant and dismissed *Doe v. Wade*. Not wanting to interfere too deeply in state affairs, the court also did not specifically prohibit the district attorney from prosecuting abortion doctors. Instead, the judges assumed that Wade would stop prosecuting them on his own since the law was now unconstitutional. In their 13-page opinion, the judges wrote,

In 1971, a rooftop billboard in Philadelphia, Pennsylvania, advertised legal abortions in New York City.

On the merits, plaintiffs argue as their principal contention that the Texas Abortion Laws must be declared unconstitutional because they deprive single women and married couples of their right, secured by the Ninth Amendment, to choose whether to have children. We agree.[7]

The judges did not find that the state's argument to protect the fetus outweighed the rights of the pregnant woman.

STARTLING REALIZATION

At the time of the *Roe v. Wade* district court decision, McCorvey was six months pregnant. Coffee called her with the news. When McCorvey asked how long the appeal would take, Coffee asked why it mattered, since an abortion had to be performed within the first 24 weeks of pregnancy. McCorvey later wrote,

> *I suddenly realized: This lawsuit was not really for me. . . . I suppose I'd always known I was too late. . . . I would have to have my baby after all.*[8]

Coffee and Weddington must have known the case would take longer than McCorvey's pregnancy. And Weddington did not tell McCorvey about the Mexican clinic where she had gone for her own abortion. In a 1994 *New York Times* interview, McCorvey spoke about Weddington:

> *Sarah sat right across the table from me at Columbo's . . . I didn't know until two years ago that she had had an abortion herself. . . . When I told her then how desperately I needed one, she could have told me where to go for it. But she wouldn't because she needed me to be pregnant for her case. . . . Sarah saw these cuts on my wrists, my swollen eyes from crying, the miserable person sitting across from her. . . . It was one of the most hideous times of my life.*[9]

Henry Wade was the defendant named in *Roe v. Wade*. The ultimate ruling on the case, made by the US Supreme Court, would make Wade's name part of US history.

Weddington and Coffee decided to appeal the *Doe* decision and the denial of a court order against the district attorney's office to stop it from prosecuting physicians who perform abortions. Attorney General Crawford Martin, the state's lead lawyer, announced the state would appeal the court's decision. Wade said publicly that his office would continue prosecuting the state abortion law. Wade's announcement would prove to be beneficial for Coffee and Weddington, as it would speed *Roe v. Wade* to the Supreme Court. ～

Chapter 7

Roe Goes to the Supreme Court

*T*he joy Coffee and Weddington felt after winning their case in district court was short-lived. Wade, Dallas County's district attorney, was not respecting the court's decision and was still prosecuting doctors who performed abortions. Essentially, nothing had changed. But Coffee and Weddington soon became aware of a procedural quirk of three-judge courts. If the court determined that a state law was unconstitutional and local authorities still enforced the law, the case could be appealed directly to the US Supreme Court. Wade had done *Roe v. Wade* a favor. Coffee and Weddington prepared appeals for both the Supreme Court and the

Linda Coffee made history with her work on *Roe v. Wade*.

Fifth Circuit Court of Appeals, in case the Supreme Court chose not to review their case.

Meanwhile, Coffee was overwhelmed with work at her regular job as a bankruptcy lawyer and Weddington was busy moving from Austin to Fort Worth to take on a new position as an assistant city attorney, as well as working on Texas abortion-reform legislation. The two lawyers had no staff or funds as they prepared the case for its next steps. When Roy Lucas, an attorney from New York, offered to help with research and fund-raising, Coffee and Weddington gladly accepted. He, too, was a new lawyer—newer than Weddington and Coffee. But he had been published in a law review arguing the unconstitutionality of abortion prohibitions, and he was willing to help.

One of Lucas's first tasks was preparing a jurisdictional statement to the Supreme Court, providing arguments why the court should hear the case. He submitted the statement on October 6, 1970. On November 5, Floyd, of the Texas

> "From personal and religious beliefs, I consider abortion an unacceptable form of population control. . . . Further unrestricted abortion policies, or abortion-on-demand, I cannot square with my personal belief in the sanctity of human life—including the life of the unborn. . . . A good and generous people will not, in my view, opt for this kind of alternative to social dilemmas. Rather, it will open its hearts and its homes to the unwanted children of its own, as it has done for the unwanted millions of other lands."[1]
>
> —RICHARD M. NIXON, US PRESIDENT, APRIL 1971

AMERICANS UNITED FOR LIFE

The first national pro-life organization, Americans United for Life (AUL), was founded in Washington DC in August 1971. Early board members were from a variety of backgrounds and included Catholics, Jews, and Unitarians. The AUL's first chairman was George Huntson Williams, a Unitarian minister who later served as a professor at Harvard Divinity School. The organization was established before *Roe* was decided, when many states were changing their abortion legislation. The AUL was created "with the goal of educating American citizenry to counter the growing threat of disrespect for human life."[2] The AUL continues to work toward this goal. In 2010, it launched Advocates for Life, a collection of pro-life student groups at law schools in the United States, including Boston College, Columbia, Harvard, and Notre Dame.

state attorney general's office, filed a response. On May 3, 1971, the Supreme Court announced it would hear *Roe v. Wade* together with an abortion case from Georgia, *Doe v. Bolton*, during its 1971 term.

Preparing for the Highest Court

In little more than a month—by June 17, 1971—Weddington and Coffee needed to file legal papers and a brief to the Supreme Court in preparation for their December court date. Lucas offered Weddington a job in a law institute he was involved with in New York that could also help her with her brief and other paperwork. She accepted and moved to New York City. But the institute had a backlog of casework and work on *Roe v. Wade* kept getting delayed. Realizing that nothing would get done unless she made it happen, Weddington put in more effort and enlisted the help of her husband and friends.

The primary argument Weddington made was that the government had never treated the fetus as a person. The Supreme Court limited briefs to 150 pages. Because 150 pages was not enough space to cover everything she and her team wanted to say, Weddington asked prominent individuals and respected organizations to write **amici curiae briefs** supporting different aspects of the case. These briefs poured in from all over the country. They came from attorneys, politicians, academics, women's groups, birth control groups, and religious organizations, including the American Jewish Congress, the Episcopal Diocese of

---

amicus curiae brief—A document filed in a court by someone not directly related to the case but who is interested and has an opinion or information about it.

New York, the United Church of Christ, and the United Methodist Church.

"The documents for *Roe* stood more than a foot high," Weddington would recall.[3] The paperwork was filed August 17, 1971, in time to meet the twice-extended deadline, and Weddington and her husband returned to Austin.

The Opposition

Tolle, the assistant district attorney from Wade's office, had hoped to stay involved in the state's response to *Roe v. Wade* and was already preparing the appeal. But Floyd informed him the state attorney general's office would now be handling the case. Just as Weddington received help with her efforts, organizations such as the National Right to Life Committee helped the state of Texas with legal counsel. More than 200 physicians opposed to ending all abortion restrictions filed amici curiae briefs, as did prominent lawyers who supported the state's position.

The defense team's task was to convince the court to reverse the lower court's ruling. Floyd asserted three points: the case was no longer valid because Roe was no longer pregnant, a woman's right to privacy has limits, and

TEXAS'S ABORTION LAW

In addition to fighting Article 1191 of Texas's penal code, *Roe v. Wade* also challenged four additional abortion-related articles:

- Article 1192. Furnishing the means: "Whoever furnishes the means for procuring an abortion knowing the purpose intended is guilty as an accomplice."

- Article 1193. Attempt at abortion: "If the means used shall fail to produce an abortion, the offender is nevertheless guilty of an attempt to produce abortion, provided it be shown that such means were calculated to produce that result, and shall be fined not less than one hundred nor more than one thousand dollars."

- Article 1194. Murder in producing abortion: "If the death of the mother is occasioned by an abortion so produced or by an attempt to effect the same it is murder."

- Article 1196. By medical advice: "Nothing in this chapter applies to an abortion procured or attempted by medical advice for the purpose of saving the life of the mother."[4]

the fetus is a human being. Rather than using a religious argument, as he had in district court, Floyd decided to base his humanness theory on science and included photographs of a developing fetus with his brief to support his position.

Oral Arguments

The oral arguments for *Roe v. Wade* were scheduled for December 13, 1971. *Doe v. Bolton* would also be argued. The companion case challenged Georgia's abortion law.

Two seats on the nine-justice court were vacant, so only seven justices were present: Warren Burger, William Brennan Jr., Byron White, William Douglas, Potter Stewart, Thurgood Marshall, and Harry Blackmun.

Douglas wrote the majority opinion in *Griswold v. Connecticut* in June 1965, which Brennan and White supported. They might be favorable toward *Roe*, although it was uncertain if they would extend the right of marital privacy to a woman's choice in abortion. Stewart voted against *Griswold* and was unlikely to favor *Roe*. The three newer justices—Marshall, Blackmun, and Burger—had not sat on the court for *Griswold*. Appointed

> " My first contested case was going to the United States Supreme Court! The little case that Linda and I had started as volunteer lawyers in response to questions from women at the referral project might well become the vehicle for protecting reproductive rights and freedom of choice for every American woman. The thought was overwhelming—and humbling."[5]
> —*SARAH WEDDINGTON, ATTORNEY FOR THE PLAINTIFF,* ROE V. WADE

by President Lyndon B. Johnson, Marshall was liberal-leaning and might be favorable. Burger and Blackmun, both Nixon appointees, were question marks. John M. Harlan and Hugo L. Black had retired, and Nixon's new appointees—Lewis F. Powell and William Rehnquist—were yet to be approved by the Senate.

After a conflict with Lucas over who should argue *Roe v. Wade*, Weddington's clients—McCorvey and the "Does"—agreed with Weddington that she should represent them. Weddington entered the back of the ornate courtroom. She would later remember that the formality of the court reminded her of walking into a church. Sharing the **appellant**'s table with her were Coffee and Lucas. Across from them sat Texas Assistant Attorney General Jay Floyd, Robert Flowers, who was Floyd's boss, and Texas Attorney General Crawford Martin. The 350-seat room was filled to capacity.

Each side in the case had 30 minutes to present. Much of that time would be spent answering the justices' questions. Weddington had practiced in mock court sessions with experienced lawyers, reviewed relevant court cases, and studied the justices' backgrounds

appellant—The person appealing a case.

THE ARGUMENT WITH LUCAS

The argument Weddington and Lucas had over who should argue the *Roe* case before the Supreme Court stemmed from Lucas's experience with the topic. He was neither more experienced nor older than Weddington. Rather, while in law school, he wrote a student law review note that was the first published argument that abortion statutes were unconstitutional. He thought that earned him the right to argue the case.

and legal views. Weddington described the impact of pregnancy on a woman's life:

> A pregnancy to a woman is perhaps one of the most determinative aspects of her life. It disrupts her body. It disrupts her education. It disrupts her employment. And it often disrupts her entire family life. And we feel that, because of the impact on the woman, this certainly in as far as there are any rights which are fundamental is a matter which is of such fundamental and basic concern to the woman involved that she should be allowed to make the choice as to whether to continue or terminate her pregnancy.[6]

Stewart asked Weddington about the constitutional basis for her clients' claims. A discussion ensued about

RIGHT TO LIFE SUNDAY

Antiabortion activists followed the *Roe v. Wade* case and other abortion-related events closely. In March 1972, the Commission on Population Growth and the American Future released a report with pro-choice recommendations. In response, New York's Cardinal Terence Cooke of the Catholic Church pronounced April 16, 1972, as Right to Life Sunday. Pro-life groups organized a rally against abortion. Lawrence Lader, a pro-choice advocate, shared his experience with the pro-life demonstrators that day:

> *The busloads unloaded on nearby streets streamed past us. They were mainly middle-aged people, prim and determined in blue serge suits and flowered Sunday dresses. When they saw our signs, their faces flushed and hardened. Most of them screamed only one word, like a small explosion, "Murderer! Murderer!" The sound rolled up the street. In that half hour, there must have been a hundred faces thrust in front of mine with the same lacerating accusation. "Murderer!" I had debated abortion hundreds of times since 1968, but never had seen so much venom concentrated at one time.*[7]

the due process and equal protection clauses of the Fourteenth Amendment. In response to a question about the history of abortion law, Weddington responded that women were not guilty of a crime for having an abortion and were seen as victims. She described the variety of ways the state did not treat the fetus as a person with legal rights, citing, for example, that abortion was not considered murder.

White asked Weddington if she made a distinction for when an abortion was performed. She replied, "No sir. . . . I feel that the question of a time limit is not strictly before the court."[8] When pressed on the issue, she said, "The Constitution, as I read it . . . attaches protection to the person at the time of birth."[9] After addressing the interests of doctors and some issues in Hallford's case, Weddington's time before the court was over.

In his opening argument for the state of Texas, Floyd asserted that the *Roe* case was no longer valid because Roe was not pregnant. He was reminded by Stewart that this was a class action and that there are "at any given time, unmarried pregnant females in the State of Texas."[10] When White asked how any woman in Texas could ever have such a case considered, Floyd replied, "I do not believe it can be done. . . . I think she makes her choice prior to the time she becomes pregnant. That is the time of choice."[11]

Under further questioning, Floyd acknowledged that Texas did not punish women for self-induced abortion, nor did any state equate aborting a developing human baby with murder. The court asked Floyd to

DOE V. BOLTON

Roe v. Wade was not the only abortion case in 1970. In Georgia, *Doe v. Bolton* had been appealed directly to the Supreme Court under circumstances similar to *Roe v. Wade*—the state was refusing to enforce the ruling of a federal court. Georgia's abortion law was modeled after the American Law Institute's *Model Penal Code*.

While Georgia's abortion law allowed abortions under more conditions than the Texas law allowed—including for the woman's health and for rape and fetal deformity—Georgia's law had complicated steps the woman needed to follow. For example, she needed to have at least two state-licensed doctors examine her and agree with her personal doctor that an abortion was necessary.

Because Georgia's abortion law was less restrictive than Texas's law, it was speculated that the Supreme Court chose to hear the two cases because they represented the abortion laws in almost every state. The decision in *Doe v. Bolton* was perhaps more important than *Roe v. Wade*, because it ruled out the possibility of an intermediate decision between nearly complete prohibition and abortion-on-demand—abortion would be allowed for any reason and during the third trimester of pregnancy.

explain why Texas barred all but a few abortions. He answered that the state had an interest in protecting fetal life. To a follow-up question from Marshall about why the state did not therefore prosecute a mother who aborted the fetus herself, Floyd conceded that the statute's original purpose was to protect the mother and not the fetus. To further questioning from Marshall on when the state attributed life to the fetus, Floyd answered, "We say there is life from the moment of impregnation."[12] Under Marshall's pointed inquiry on the timing of life, Floyd finally said, "Mr. Justice, there are unanswerable questions in this field."[13] Floyd concluded his 30-minute argument by saying, "We think these matters are matters of policy which can be properly addressed by the State legislature. We think that a consideration should be given to the unborn."[14]

After the attorneys for and against *Doe v. Bolton* presented their oral arguments concerning Georgia's abortion law, the court session was finished. Three days later, the justices convened in private conference to discuss the case. The attorneys—and the nation—awaited the court's decision. ～

Reargument
and a Decision

On June 26, 1972, the Supreme Court sent notice that *Roe v. Wade* and *Doe v. Bolton* were "restored to the calendar for reargument."[1] Although no reason was given for why the cases were to be heard again, it is assumed that the justices wanted the decision to come from a full nine-member court—the Senate had only recently confirmed Justices Powell and Rehnquist. It is also conjectured that Blackmun, the justice writing the majority opinion, wanted more time to craft his response.

The attorneys for both sides of *Roe v. Wade* returned to the Supreme Court on October 11, 1972. Arguing again for *Roe*, Weddington added evidence

Sarah Weddington and Linda Coffee's challenge
to Texas's abortion laws took them to the Supreme Court,
where their argument ultimately changed US abortion laws.

from recently decided cases favorable to abortion and the
statistic that more than 1,600 Texas women had traveled
to New York to take advantage of that state's more liberal
abortion laws. In her closing remarks, Weddington said,

> We do not ask this Court to rule that abortion is
> good, or desirable in any particular situation. We
> are here to advocate that the decision as to whether
> or not a particular woman will continue to carry
> or will terminate a pregnancy is a decision that
> should be made by that individual.[2]

Flowers replaced Floyd in arguing for the defendant. He argued two points. First, the state had an interest in protecting the fetus from conception. Second, balancing a mother's right to privacy with the interest of the fetus was best left to the state legislature. When asked about the constitutional definition of the word *personhood*, Flowers replied,

> *Your Honor, it is our position that the definition of a person is so basic . . . so fundamental that the framers of the Constitution had not even set out to define it.*[3]

After further questioning, the second round of arguments concluded. Again, all that was left to do was wait. It would be more than three months before the justices' ruling would be known.

The Decision

On January 22, 1973, the Supreme Court announced to a courtroom packed with onlookers and reporters that, by a vote of seven to two, they had ruled the Texas abortion law unconstitutional. Coffee heard about the decision in her car driving to work. Weddington was in her office when she heard the news. "I could hardly believe that at twenty-seven years of age I had won an important Supreme Court case," Weddington would recall.[4] While thrilled with the results, and amid a media frenzy and celebrations, the lawyers were left to wonder about the ruling—its exact wording and which justices were for or against *Roe*.

The details came to light the following day. Blackmun, who wrote the majority opinion, ruled in favor of *Roe*, as did Brennan, Burger, Douglas, Marshall, Powell, and Stewart. White and Rehnquist **dissented**.

Majority Opinion

In crafting his majority opinion, Blackmun spent a great deal of time on medical and historical research. He was impressed with the ideas that abortion laws were originally meant to protect the woman's health and not the fetus; that with new surgical techniques, abortion was a much safer procedure than it used to be; and that the fetus had not historically been granted the legal status of being a person. In fact, most of Blackmun's historical propositions were wrong, but they became the basis for the decision. He proposed that pregnancy be

dissent—To disagree with the majority decision in a court case.

The US Supreme Court justices who ruled on *Roe v. Wade*

divided into trimesters, though the concept had not been brought up by either side of the case and was not based on constitutional law. This division of pregnancy would become a sticking point as the justices considered on the opinion. The court's final majority opinion spelled out several main points. First, the direct appeal of *Roe v. Wade* to the Supreme Court was proper. In addition, Roe had **standing to sue**, and the fact that she was no longer pregnant did not affect her status as a plaintiff. Regarding the cases bundled with *Roe*, the Does and Hallford did not have standing to sue. However, the overall ruling would free Hallford from the criminal charges against him.

Regarding the Fourteenth Amendment, Texas's abortion law violated the due process clause, which protects a person's right to privacy from state action. This included a woman's right to end her pregnancy. On this point, Blackmun wrote,

> *The Constitution does not explicitly mention any right of privacy. In a line of decisions, however . . . the Court has recognized that a right of personal privacy, or a guarantee of certain areas or zones of privacy, does exist under the Constitution. . . . This right of privacy . . . is broad enough to encompass a woman's decision whether or not to terminate her pregnancy.*[5]

Based on historical and legal **precedents**, the court did not agree with the state's assertion that Fourteenth Amendment privacy protections extended to the unborn. In addition, the state had a legitimate interest in protecting a pregnant woman's health but also the potentiality of human life. Here, the Supreme Court

precedent—A court ruling or decision that becomes an example and is noted in later rulings in similar cases.

standing to sue—The ability of a person or group of people to show the court that the person or group will suffer harm as a result of the law or laws being challenged.

disagreed with Weddington's argument that a woman's right was absolute. Blackmun addressed the matter:

> It is reasonable and appropriate for a State to decide that, at some point in time another interest, that of the mother or that of potential human life, becomes significantly involved. The woman's privacy is no longer sole and any right of privacy she possesses must be measured accordingly.[6]

He added, "With respect to the State's important and legitimate interest in potential life, the 'compelling' point is at viability."[7] And regarding the hotly contested issue of when life begins, Blackmun wrote,

> We need not resolve the difficult question of when life begins. When those trained in the respective disciplines of medicine, philosophy, and theology are unable to arrive at any consensus, the judiciary . . . is not in a position to speculate as to the answer.[8]

In an unusual move, Blackmun added a **dictum** to the decision. In it, he advised states on how to regulate abortion. Blackmun based his advice on his trimester approach. In the first trimester, the abortion decision should be left up to the woman upon advice of her doctor. In the second trimester, the state could impose regulations related to maternal health. In the last trimester, the state could regulate or deny abortion, as long as it did not harm the life or health of the mother. In fact, these standards were not simply dictum but the **holding**— any statute that did not conform to the trimester scheme would be unconstitutional.

> "We forthwith acknowledge our awareness of the sensitive and emotional nature of the abortion controversy, of the vigorous opposing views, even among physicians, and of the deep and seemingly absolute convictions that the subject inspires. One's philosophy, one's experiences, one's exposure to the raw edges of human experience, one's religious training, one's attitudes toward life and family and their values, and the moral standards one establishes and seeks to observe, are all likely to influence and to color one's thinking and conclusions about abortion."[9]
>
> —*JUSTICE HARRY BLACKMUN, DELIVERING THE MAJORITY OPINION, ROE V. WADE, JANUARY 22, 1973*

Three justices wrote concurring opinions. Burger, the chief justice, noted his concern over the court's extensive use of medical and scientific data in reaching its opinion. Douglas delved into the idea of fetal life, writing, "To say

---

dictum—A judge's expressed opinion on a point other than the exact issue involved in deciding a case.

holding—The ruling on a case.

that life is present at conception is to give recognition to the potential, rather than the actual. . . . The law does not deal in speculation."[10] Stewart noted concern with the appropriateness of the trimester advice, since no such state law was at issue before the court.

The Dissents

White strongly disagreed with the majority. In his dissent, White wrote,

> *The Court for the most part sustains this position: During the period prior to the time the fetus becomes viable, the Constitution of the United State values the convenience, whim or caprice of the [hypothetical] mother more than the life or potential life of the fetus. . . .*
>
> *With all due respect, I dissent. I find nothing in the language or history of the Constitution to support the Court's judgment.*[11]

Arguing for state's rights, White called the court's decision "an exercise of raw judicial power" and an "extravagant exercise of the power of judicial review."[12] He added, "This issue . . . should be left with the people and to the political processes the people have devised to govern their affairs."[13]

OPINIONS AND DISSENTS

A Supreme Court opinion is the written justification for the court's majority ruling on a case. A dissent is a written disagreement with the majority. Opinions are written by one justice and carry the name of that single author, but a majority of justices must agree by signing or joining the opinion before the ruling is publicly delivered. Because a justice may switch his or her vote anytime during the deliberation process, opinions are a group effort, filled with discussions and compromise. If a justice sides with the majority but is unhappy with the written opinion, he or she may write a concurring opinion to explain his or her own thoughts. Since a justice writing a dissenting or concurring opinion is not writing for the court as a whole, these documents are often much more personal and individual.

In addition to joining White's dissent, Rehnquist wrote a dissent of his own. In it, he noted that the Supreme Court "was saying that a state could impose very few restrictions in the first trimester."[14] He went on to question how far along in her pregnancy Roe was when the suit was filed. Perhaps the stage of pregnancy would have limited Roe to being granted an abortion only to save her life. Regardless of knowing the stage of Roe's pregnancy, Rehnquist was firm in his minority opinion:

MCCORVEY LEARNS ABOUT THE RULING

According to Weddington, she tried to get in touch with McCorvey after the Supreme Court's ruling but was unable to reach her. McCorvey wrote about learning the outcome of her case while reading the newspaper:

> I sat at the kitchen table, drinking a beer and reading . . . my eyes wandered to the lower right-hand corner of the page. There was a small, matter-of-fact article that said that the United States Supreme Court had legalized abortion all over the United States. . . . For a long while I just stared into space, fighting my emotions.[16]

> *A transaction resulting in an operation such as this is not "private" in the ordinary usage of that word. Nor is the "privacy" that the Court finds here even a distant relative of the freedom from searches and seizures protected by the Fourth Amendment to the Constitution, which the Court has referred to as embodying a right to privacy.*[15]

The woman is not alone during an abortion, since the doctor and unborn child are with her, so the matter is not private. Rehnquist also contended that the very existence of a widespread abortion debate showed that abortion was not universally accepted.

The Supreme Court's ruling in *Roe v. Wade* overruled the "unreformed" abortion statutes across the United States. In addition to ruling in favor of *Roe*, the justices ruled in favor of *Doe* in *Doe v. Bolton*, the Georgia case they heard along with *Roe*. The *Doe* case overruled what *Roe* did not, striking down the *Model Penal Code*, which Georgia followed, and ruling out the possibility of any compromise. In his opinion, Blackmun used the same rationale he used in *Roe*, but he also ruled the hurdles the Georgia abortion law required women to jump over invalid, including approval for an abortion from a hospital abortion committee. As they had done in *Roe*, White and Rehnquist dissented in *Doe v. Bolton*.

The ruling left 31 states without any abortion laws and other states with laws not in complete compliance. While some state legislatures quickly went to work rewriting their abortion legislation, others simply declared their laws unconstitutional or issued statements that they could be ignored.

While the *Roe* ruling was a singular decision that applied to the nation, it did not unite the country. The court's decision only intensified the abortion controversy. Fierce battles over *Roe* were soon to come. ∼

Chapter 9

Early Challenges to *Roe*

Criticism of the *Roe v. Wade* ruling was immediate and widespread. Liberals and conservatives alike believed Blackmun's opinion was too broad. John Hart Ely, a constitutional scholar and law professor in favor of abortion rights, did not believe the Constitution specifically provided for a right to privacy and did believe abortion laws were best left to legislators to decide. Ruth Bader Ginsburg, head of the American Civil Liberties Union's Women's Rights Project, thought the ruling stopped the government from intruding on a fundamental liberty in terms of the Fourteenth Amendment's due process clause. However, many poor, young, unmarried,

The court's decision on *Roe* sparked protests immediately, including a march at the capitol in St. Paul, Minnesota, the day of the ruling.

ABORTION STATISTICS AT THE TIME OF *ROE V. WADE*

It is difficult to know how many American women ended their pregnancies with abortion prior to the decision in *Roe v. Wade* in 1973, since illegal abortions were a hidden procedure and accurate records were not kept. In the late 1950s, the Alfred Kinsey Foundation estimated 1.2 million abortions were performed annually, though their survey subjects were all white and upper-middle class. It seems unlikely that any large number of women continued to use illegal abortions once it became legal everywhere in the United States. In 1973, almost 616,000 legal abortions were performed.[1] By 1975, after abortion had been legal across the nation for two years, the Centers for Disease Control and Prevention has estimated there were 1 million abortions performed annually.[2]

and minority women were still left unable to obtain abortions because of their circumstances.

Moral, Religious, and Political Opposition

In addition to concerns over its legal soundness, *Roe v. Wade* was condemned on personal and moral grounds. Many people were outraged that abortion-on-demand had essentially become the law of the land. The most vocal and structured opposition to the ruling came from organized religion, beginning with the Roman Catholic Church, which believes in the sanctity of life. This doctrine holds that all life, including that of an unborn child, is precious in all circumstances. Cardinal John Krol, president of the National Catholic Conference, said the *Roe* decision was allowing the "greatest slaughter of innocent life in the history of mankind."[3] In 1975, the National Conference of Catholic Bishops called for a grassroots effort to change public policy and campaign for a Constitutional amendment to ban abortion. Protestant denominations, particularly fundamental and evangelical churches, also denounced the *Roe* ruling.

The loose coalition of individuals and groups making up what was becoming known as the pro-life movement would continue to grow. In 1979, the

PRO-LIFE AND PRO-CHOICE

Individuals and groups opposed to abortion began referring to themselves as "pro-life" to focus on their commitment to the unborn fetus and to emphasize that abortion takes the life of a child. The term was coined in 1973.

Individuals and groups in favor of abortion rights prefer to call themselves "pro-choice" to emphasize their commitment to a woman's right to choose abortion, rather than support of abortion itself.

CHRISTIAN DIRECTIVES

The Roman Catholic Church teaches that life starts at conception and that to destroy a developing human baby at any stage of pregnancy, whether an embryo or fetus, for any reason, is morally wrong. In 1995, Pope John Paul II explained the church's position in the *Evangelium Vitae 62*:

> *I declare that direct abortion . . . always constitutes a grave moral disorder, since it is the deliberate killing of an innocent human being. This doctrine is based upon the natural law and upon the written word of God, is transmitted by the Church's tradition and taught by the ordinary and universal [teaching authority of the church]. No circumstance, no purpose, no law whatsoever can ever make licit an act which is intrinsically illicit, since it is contrary to the law of God which is written in every human heart, knowable by reason itself, and proclaimed by the Church.*[4]

Evangelical Christians tend to focus their pro-life arguments on the Bible, including Genesis 1:28, which guides people to "be fruitful and increase in number" and Psalms 139:13–16, which refers to God knowing individuals in the womb.[5]

National Right to Life Committee had 11 million members in more than 1,800 affiliate organizations. Due in large part to pro-life lobbying efforts, sympathetic members of Congress would submit a number of human life amendment bills after the *Roe v. Wade* ruling. But no bill had enough congressional or public support to pass. One victory was the Hyde Amendment, passed in 1976, which prevented Medicaid funds from being spent on abortions, except to save the life of the mother or in cases of rape or incest.

In addition to their lobbying efforts for pro-life legislation, right-to-life members campaigned for political candidates who shared their values. With significant help from pro-life supporters, Republican Ronald Reagan was elected president in 1980. As president, Reagan would nominate three Supreme Court justices: Anthony Kennedy, Sandra Day O'Connor, and Antonin Scalia. Because a predominantly liberal court had ruled in favor of *Roe v. Wade*, people opposed to abortion knew that placing more conservatives on the bench was a key step in overturning the ruling.

Opposition to *Roe* Turns Violent

Frustrated with the slow action in reinstating abortion laws, some pro-life activists began using confrontational and violent tactics. By 1988, 77 family planning and abortion clinics had been bombed, 117 had been burned, 250 had received bomb threats, 231 had been

Some people have used violence and destruction
to express their feelings about abortion.

burglarized, and 224 had been vandalized. A member of
the Army of God group claimed responsibility in 1984
for four arson attacks in Washington State, saying he
had done it "for the glory of God."[6] Joseph Scheidler, a
pro-life protest organizer at the time, said of the violent
protests, "We understand why it occurs. Still, I reject it.

I don't think it is helpful, or that it will work to change anything. We prefer persuasion."[7]

In 1984, Randall Terry was working as a car salesman when he began picketing abortion clinics. In 1986, he created a group called Operation Rescue through which he organized abortion clinic protests involving hundreds of pro-life volunteers. In addition to sit-ins, Operation Rescue members would jam entryways and chain themselves to doors to keep providers and patients from entering. Members known as sidewalk counselors would talk to arriving patients. Many protestors were arrested. Operation Rescue attracted thousands of followers, primarily evangelical Christians. By the late 1980s, the organization had nearly shut down abortion clinics in Los Angeles, New York City, and Atlanta. Terry left Operation Rescue after incurring massive legal debt. He later returned to the organization, which continues under different leadership.

State Laws and Legal Challenges

Through the 1970s and into the late 1980s, Americans generally favored abortion rights, but they also favored more regulation than allowed by *Roe v. Wade* and *Doe v. Bolton*. One poll showed that more than 75 percent of respondents favored parental notification and consent requirements for minors.[8] Six months after the *Roe v. Wade* decision, 188 pro-life laws were introduced in 41 states.[9] By 1983, the Supreme Court would hear and decide on 15 cases challenging state abortion laws.[10]

While the court found in favor of states seeking to restrict funding for abortions, the justices were more cautious with restrictions that hindered a woman from obtaining an abortion. In early rulings, the Supreme Court struck down state laws requiring a husband's consent before his wife could get an abortion, as well as requirements that doctors read a pro-life script to patients and that patients be hospitalized in the second trimester of pregnancy.

Roe v. Wade received its first major Supreme Court challenge in the 1989 case *Webster v. Reproductive Health Services*, in which the state of Missouri asked that *Roe* be overturned. On July 3, the court upheld some restrictions of Missouri's pre-*Roe* pro-life law, such as testing for fetal viability, but it did not overturn *Roe*.

The next major challenge came on June 29, 1992, with the ruling on *Planned Parenthood of Southeastern Pennsylvania v. Casey*. This case challenged Pennsylvania's Abortion Control Act. The law contained abortion requirements, including patient-informed consent, a 24-hour waiting period, spousal notification, and parental consent for minors. By 1992, the Supreme Court was considerably different than it was in 1973. The bench now had eight justices appointed by Republican presidents, and the only remaining Democratic appointee—Byron White—had been a dissenter on the *Roe* decision.

CONSTRUCTIONISM AND THE RIGHT OF PRIVACY

Constructionism refers to a belief in the way the Constitution should be read. Loose constructionists believe the Constitution should take modern thinking into account. Strict constructionists believe the Constitution should be approached through the thinking and values held by the Founding Fathers and not subject to changing values.

One criticism of the *Roe v. Wade* decision involves the right of privacy and whether that right exists in the Constitution. Those opposed to this legal aspect of the ruling in the case tend to be strict constructionists. The Constitution contains no word or phrase saying there is a right to privacy, therefore, there can be no subsequent right to abortion. Loose constructionists point out that vital rights, such as those for the woman's vote, came from an interpretation of the underlying values of the Constitution, not from its exact words.

The result in the *Casey* ruling was mixed. In a 5–4 decision, the court upheld *Roe v. Wade*'s basic premise that women had a right to abortion and that abortions could not be banned in the early stages of pregnancy. The court refused to overturn *Roe* based on **stare decisis**. In her majority opinion for *Casey*, O'Connor wrote,

> *A decision to overrule* Roe*'s essential holding under the existing circumstances would address error, if error there was, at the cost of both profound and unnecessary damage to the Court's legitimacy and to the Nation's commitment to the rule of law.*[11]

While the court upheld *Roe* in its ruling on *Casey*, the justices did overturn Blackmun's trimester concept and declare that states should have more leeway in deciding when a fetus was viable. This was an important note since, according to *Roe*, states could refuse an abortion if a fetus were viable. States could impose abortion restrictions as long as the restrictions did not create undue obstacles for a woman seeking an abortion—a lesser legal standard than *Roe* required.

stare decisis—A policy of deciding a case based on previous court decisions unless they violate the ordinary principles of justice.

MCCORVEY HARASSED

After allowing her identity as Jane Roe to be revealed in a made-for-television movie aired in 1989, McCorvey became a victim of harassment. She described her experience:

> *The first pieces of hate mail began to find their way to our mailbox. The letters were usually scrawled, mostly misspelled, on school notebook paper with Magic Marker or pencil. They weren't signed. They called me a baby killer, evil, and much, much worse. These letters chilled my blood.*[12]

For the most part, the principles of *Roe v. Wade* were upheld by the Supreme Court in the *Casey* decision. However, with two justices nearing retirement and a Republican president running for reelection, many believed it was simply a matter of time before *Roe* would fail being challenged. ～

Chapter 10

Roe's Broad Shadow

*I*n *Webster v. Reproductive Health Services* (1989) and in *Planned Parenthood of Southeastern Pennsylvania v. Casey* (1992), the Supreme Court alerted those sympathetic to abortion rights that *Roe* was vulnerable. After the Supreme Court's ruling in *Casey*, states began passing more restrictive abortion laws.

The chances of *Roe* being overturned by the Supreme Court became less likely with the election of Democrat Bill Clinton, who was pro-choice, in 1992. His court appointments of Ruth Bader Ginsburg and Stephen Breyer ensured *Roe* would remain intact for at least a while longer. However, while Clinton was in office, the Republican Congress banned abortions on US military bases. Under the law, the procedure was allowed when the pregnancy was the result of rape or incest, or when the mother's life was in jeopardy.

In 2000, the Supreme Court overruled a Nebraska law banning partial-birth abortions because the law was too vague. The 5–4 vote in this case, *Stenberg v. Carhart*, was close. This outcome was encouraging to pro-life advocates. And in 2007, the court upheld a nearly identical case: *Gonzalez v. Carhart*.

Abortion Violence Escalates

While the issue of abortion continued to be fought in courts, there was a literal battle beyond the courtrooms. The early 1990s saw an increase in violence toward doctors who performed abortions. On March 10, 1993, David Gunn became the first doctor murdered for performing abortions when he was shot to death during a pro-life rally in Pensacola, Florida. In August that same year, Doctor George Tiller was shot by a woman attending a pro-life rally outside an abortion clinic in Wichita, Kansas. The next day, George Patterson, a physician who owned four abortion clinics in the

David Gunn Jr. spoke on Capitol Hill after his father, a doctor, was killed outside an abortion clinic.

southeast, was murdered. In July 1994, another doctor, John Britton, was murdered outside a Pensacola, Florida, abortion clinic by a former evangelical minister. Britton's security escort, James H. Barrett, was also killed, and Barrett's wife was badly injured. The perpetrators and some of their supporters justified the killings by saying

116

that abortionists were murderers. Most in the pro-life community strongly denounced the violence.

As a result of these and other attacks and abortion-clinic blockades, pro-choice organizations filed lawsuits in federal and state courts seeking injunctions against pro-life protestors and to seek buffer zones between protestors and people entering and leaving clinics. In 1993, Congress passed the Freedom of Access to Clinic Entrances Act. Signed into law on May 26, 1994, it made interfering with people accessing or providing reproductive care unlawful. In 2000, the Supreme Court ruled in *Hill v. Colorado* that Colorado could require a protective zone of eight feet (2 m) between protestors and people entering and exiting health-care facilities.

Bush Brings Change

In 2000, Republican George W. Bush was elected president with the help of pro-life forces. One of his first acts after taking office in 2001 was signing an executive order blocking US funds for international family-planning groups that either offered abortion or provided abortion counseling. The rule had been in place under Republican presidents Reagan and George H. W. Bush, but it had been changed by Clinton.

After the 2002 midterm elections, Republicans were in charge of the White House and both houses of Congress for the first time since the *Roe v. Wade* decision. In 2003, Congress passed a ban on late-term abortions. Bush signed the Partial-Birth Abortion Ban Act into law on November 5, 2003.

In July 2003, Wanda Franz, president of the National Right to Life Committee, said of pro-life successes, "I think you could say that we're at our strongest since *Roe v. Wade*."[1] Franz was not exactly right, but the numbers were close. A 2003 Gallup Poll indicated that 45 percent of Americans considered themselves pro-life, while 48 percent identified themselves as pro-choice.[2]

Opinions about *Roe v. Wade* and abortion were mixed. In 2003, the thirtieth anniversary of the landmark ruling, a USA Today/CNN/Gallup poll showed that 53 percent of Americans thought *Roe* was a "good thing" for the country, 30 percent considered it a "bad thing," and 17 percent of respondents were "uncertain."[3] Another poll revealed interesting statistics about women's opinion on abortion. A poll showed that many women were not in favor of the procedure. Fifty-one percent of women polled responded that abortion

EMBRYONIC STEM-CELL AND FETAL TISSUE RESEARCH

After taking office in 2001, George W. Bush limited federal funding for fetal-tissue and embryonic stem-cell research. When Barack Obama took office in January 2009, he reversed this move.

Stem cells from human embryos can turn into any specialized cell, such as skin, bone, or blood. They are valued for research into chronic health conditions. Stem cells replace damaged cells and repair the damage. While stem cells offer great hope for curing diseases, human embryos are destroyed in the research process, which is troubling for those who believe life starts at conception.

Stem-cell research has never been banned in the United States, but the federal government passed regulations five years after the *Roe* decision barring the use of federal research funds on experiments using human embryos, fetuses, and fetal tissue. In 2011, Congress introduced a bill to allow federal funding by statute.

Scientists have been using fetal tissue in research for an even longer period than stem cells. Unlike stem cells, which are usually taken from leftover fertility-clinic embryos, fetal tissue is often taken from aborted fetuses. Those opposed to fetal-tissue research believe it promotes and legitimizes abortion.

should be allowed only in cases of rape, incest, or life-threatening situations, and 30 percent thought abortion should be generally available.[4] The following year, one

PRO-CHOICE REPUBLICANS AND PRO-LIFE DEMOCRATS

Not all Democrats are pro-choice, and not all Republicans are pro-life. Members of Democrats for Life of America, for example, believe in core Democratic values and that "the protection of human life is the foundation of human rights, authentic freedom, and good government."[5] They oppose capital punishment and genocide in addition to abortion and other life-endangering issues. The organization Republican Majority for Choice is made up of Republican men and women who are pro-choice. According to the organization's Web site, members "believe that personal and medical decisions are best made between a woman, her doctor, and her family and out of the hands of government."[6] In a June 2011 Gallup Poll, 27 percent of Republicans identified themselves as pro-choice and 32 percent of Democrats said they were pro-life.[7]

family's tragedy would become a national event and put *Roe*'s arguments about rights to life and privacy in the spotlight with regard to the end of life.

Terri Schiavo

In 2005, Terri Schiavo was in her fifteenth year of being in an irreversible coma. Her parents, Robert and Mary Schindler, believed she was still conscious. Schiavo's husband, Michael, argued that she never wanted to be kept alive artificially and should be allowed to die. Although Terri did not have a living will, her husband **testified** in court that she had told him in conversations that she would not want to be kept alive artificially. Her family disputed his **testimony**. A Florida court ruled in his favor and Terri's feeding tube was removed. She died 13 days later, on March 31, 2005.

The case caught the attention of right-to-life groups, many of them the same organizations involved in the pro-life movement. The National Right to Life Committee argued that protecting the end of life was as important as protecting life in the womb, and they helped draft a bill for Congress allowing the Schindlers to appeal their case in federal court. Others believed that, as in *Roe v. Wade*, the Constitution's guarantee of individual privacy extended to a person's right to die. The case brought up bioethical questions concerning euthanasia and the importance of the quality of life versus the sanctity of life, an argument that continues today.

testified—Declared something in court under oath.
testimony—Something declared in court under oath.

Shifting Court and Political Landscape

While in office, Bush appointed two justices: John Roberts and Samuel Alito, to replace Rehnquist and O'Connor, respectively. The Supreme Court again appeared aligned to overturn *Roe v. Wade*. In 2006, the Supreme Court heard two cases challenging the federal ban on partial-birth abortions: *Gonzales v. Carhart* and *Gonzales v. Planned Parenthood*. O'Connor had generally favored women's rights issues and had a mixed record on abortion. Without her vote, the court ruled in April 2007 to uphold the federal ban in a 5–4 decision.

In 2008, a Democratic pro-choice candidate— Barack Obama—was elected president. Among Obama's first actions as president was signing an executive order in January 2009 re-allowing abortion on military bases. Obama also restored funds for organizations providing

NO FEDERAL MONEY FOR ABORTIONS

In March 2010, after a yearlong battle between President Obama and federal legislators, Congress passed a comprehensive health-care reform bill, the Affordable Care Act, overhauling the nation's health system. The final deal that ensured its passage was an agreement with Democratic abortion opponents that federal money in the bill could not be used for abortions.

HEALTH RISKS OF ABORTION

According to the Guttmacher Institute, a nonprofit pro-choice reproductive research and policy group, less than three-tenths of one percent of abortion patients have complications that require hospitalization. When performed in the first trimester of pregnancy, abortion poses little long-term risk of infertility, miscarriage, birth defects, or preterm deliveries. There is one death per every 1 million abortions at or before the eighth week of pregnancy and one death per every 29,000 abortions at or after the twenty-first week of pregnancy.[8]

In February 2012, the journal *Obstetrics & Gynecology* reported on the safety of legal abortions compared to that of childbirth. In "The Comparative Safety of Legal Induced Abortion and Childbirth in the United States," doctors Elizabeth G. Raymond and David A. Grimes conclude,

Legal induced abortion is markedly safer than childbirth. The risk of death associated with childbirth is approximately 14 times higher than that with abortion. Similarly, the overall morbidity associated with childbirth exceeds that with abortion.[9]

overseas abortions and abortion counseling. More than 30 years after the *Roe* ruling, these presidents' actions reflected the continued division in Americans' beliefs about abortion. ~

Chapter 11

Abortion Today
and the Future
of *Roe*

ccording to a 2011 report by the US Census
Bureau, abortions decreased from 1.6 million
performed in 1990 to 1.2 million in 2006.[1] Reasons
offered for the drop include greater acceptance
of unmarried women giving birth, greater use of
contraception, and fewer unintended pregnancies.
Other reasons may be an increase in the percentage
of older, non-childbearing women in the country.
Finally, state laws restricting or discouraging abortion
and lack of availability of abortion providers may have

contributed to the decrease in abortions over that
time period.

State Abortion Statutes

As of early 2012, at least 39 states had placed limits on
how late abortions could be performed, with at least
seven of these states banning abortions after the twentieth
week of pregnancy or requiring physicians to test for

RECENT ABORTION STATISTICS

According to statistics reported by the Guttmacher
Institute in August 2011, almost half of American women's
pregnancies are unintended. Approximately 40 percent of
these unintended pregnancies are terminated by abortion.
Of all pregnancies except miscarriages, 22 percent end in
abortion. In 2008, 1.21 million abortions were performed.
This was a decrease from 1.31 million in 2000. Regarding
who has abortions, 42 percent of women who have the
procedure have incomes below the poverty level. By
age group, women in their twenties have more than 50
percent of all abortions. Young women ages 18–19 have 11
percent of all abortions, teens 15–17 have 6 percent, and
teens younger than 15 have 0.4 percent. According to the
institute's report,

> At least half of American women will experience an
> unintended pregnancy by age 45, and, at current
> rates, one in 10 women will have an abortion by age
> 20, one in four by age 30 and three in 10 by age 45.[2]

viability. At least 37 states enforced some kind of parental consent or notification laws for minors seeking an abortion. Most of these laws gave minors an alternative to parental consent, such as a court authorization.

Some state abortion restrictions have discouraged women from following through with their abortions. At least 19 states required women to receive counseling before they could have the procedure. In at least 24 states, a woman was required to wait, usually 24 hours, between receiving counseling and having the abortion performed. At least 20 states had enacted laws that require or encourage a woman to have an ultrasound prior to an abortion.

Lack of Providers

In addition to the variety of restrictive state abortion laws decreasing the abortion rate, between 1992 and 2000, there was a 17 percent reduction in the number of abortion providers.[3] This decrease was a result of training and legislature.

Few medical-school residency programs provide training in abortion procedures, and few young physicians are taking the places of retiring abortion providers. In addition, at least 46 states allow health-care

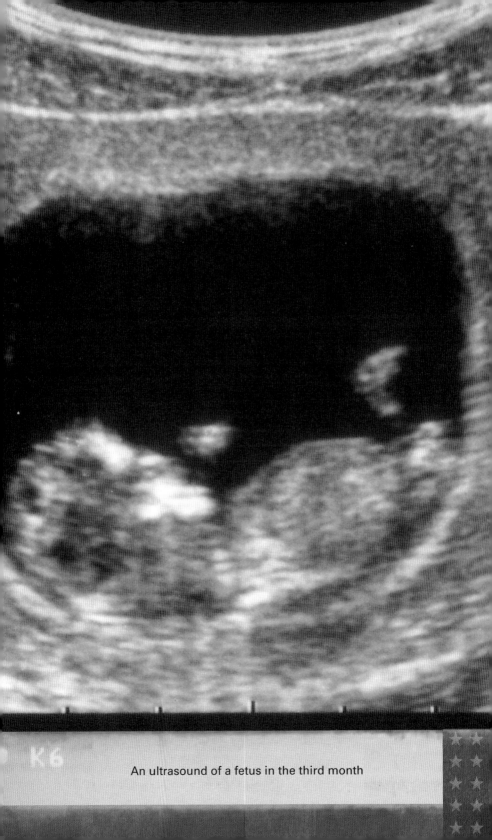

K6

An ultrasound of a fetus in the third month

providers not to participate in abortions. A few states, such as Kansas, have laws regulating abortion clinics that are so restrictive that few or no clinics in those states are able to meet the licensing requirements.

Mifepristone (RU 486)

Pharmaceutical advances have also played a role in abortions. In September 2000, the US Food and Drug Administration approved a drug that some hoped would make abortion simpler and place it more under the pregnant woman's control. Mifepristone, a drug formerly known as RU 486, is used alone and with the drug misoprostol to induce abortion in the early stages of pregnancy. According to Planned Parenthood, it is distributed by physicians, requires at least two visits to a doctor, can be used within 63 days of the woman's last period, and is about 97 percent effective.[4] Some clinics offer only medication abortions.

But mifepristone is not the abortion panacea some thought it might become. In addition to the required visits to a doctor, it can be as expensive as a surgical abortion—$300 to $800 for the drug, compared with $300 to $950 for the procedure—and the pain or discomfort can last several days. By 2008, mifepristone

SARAH WEDDINGTON: POLITICIAN, PROFESSOR, AND SPEAKER

Happy with her initial appearance at the Supreme Court but unsure if the justices would decide in favor of *Roe v. Wade*, Weddington lobbied for abortion reform legislation in her home state of Texas. Frustrated with a lack of legislative progress, and thinking she could more easily effect change from inside the government, she announced her candidacy for the state House of Representatives on February 7, 1972. On November 7, 1972, at the age of 27, Weddington became the first woman elected from Travis County to the Texas House of Representatives.

After successfully concluding her appeal of *Roe v. Wade* in the Supreme Court, Weddington became president of the National Association for the Repeal of Abortion Laws. She was elected for two more terms in the Texas House of Representatives and served as general counsel for the US Department of Agriculture under President Jimmy Carter. Weddington wrote about her *Roe* experiences in *A Question of Choice*, published in 1992. As of 2009, Weddington was a professor at the University of Texas and a speaker on reproductive rights and other women's issues.

accounted for approximately 25 percent of all abortions before nine weeks' pregnancy.[5] Mifepristone is contentious for most of the same reasons as abortion—the US approval process took 20 years because of opposition. And, though many abortion laws were

HENRY WADE

Henry Wade, the named defendant in *Roe v. Wade*, died in 2001 at the age of 86 after more than 35 years as district attorney of Dallas County, Texas, from 1951 to 1987. He never lost a case that he personally prosecuted. Upon his death, the *New York Times* noted,

> Mr. Wade's cigar chewing, his drawl, his love of dominoes and his puttering around his farm near Dallas gave him an artfully deceiving image. His folksy manner masked a keen legal mind, a fiercely competitive streak and a relentless faith in the efficacy of punishment.[6]

created before medical abortion was available, these laws still apply to the practice. Some states have passed laws specifically restricting its use. Deaths and injuries have been attributed to the drug, most of them when it has not been taken as directed.

Will *Roe v. Wade* Be Overturned?

While *Roe v. Wade* continues to exist, it has not gone unchallenged or unchanged. A few factors could determine if it is eventually overturned, or reversed, by a Supreme Court ruling. The makeup of the Supreme Court is continually shifting as justices retire and are replaced by the president in office. As of 2012, five

130

of the sitting justices were selected by Republican presidents and four by Democratic presidents. A change in that balance could affect *Roe*'s status.

If *Roe v. Wade* were overturned, it might come in the form of a ban or lawsuit brought by a group challenging an existing state abortion law. For example, several states currently ban late-term abortions after the twentieth week of pregnancy. These laws violate *Roe v. Wade*, which set the limit at 24 to 28 weeks, but none of the laws has been challenged in federal court.

If the Supreme Court agrees to hear a case to reverse *Roe v. Wade*, the justices might determine that a constitutional right of privacy does not extend to a woman's right to terminate a pregnancy. Or they might defer to states' rights. Justice Thomas, for example, has said that the Constitution may permit a state to allow abortion, but it does not require states to do so. Or the justices might determine the fetus is a person with constitutional rights deserving legal protection.

Fetal Rights and Fetal Personhood

When *Roe v. Wade* was decided in 1973, the Supreme Court majority determined—based on its interpretation of legal precedent—that the fetus did not have full legal status until birth. Scientific insight into human pregnancy has been providing evidence that the fetus shows life at increasingly earlier stages. In the third trimester of pregnancy, the fetus has full brain activity and seems to feel a variety of sensations. At six to eight weeks, the fetal nervous system has electric activity and a heartbeat can be detected. Medical advances keep pushing up the point of viability.

Armed with this compelling evidence, pro-life supporters have helped pass fetal-protection—feticide—laws in at least 38 states that make the unprovoked killing of a fetus by violent acts against a pregnant woman a homicide. On April 1, 2004, the Unborn Victims of Violence Act became law, making it a separate crime to kill a fetus in the course of committing certain **federal crimes**. Pro-choice supporters fear that laws recognizing the personhood of the fetus could be interpreted to include a woman's unhealthy or risky behavior during pregnancy and could also provide potential legal precedent for overturning *Roe v. Wade*.

federal crime—A crime that breaks a US federal law rather than a state or local law.

2011 GALLUP POLLS ON ABORTION

Polls on abortion often reveal conflicting feelings and beliefs among respondents. In a May 2011 Gallup Poll, 49 percent of Americans called themselves pro-choice, while 45 percent identified themselves pro-life. The poll found that 51 percent of Americans believe abortion is morally wrong, while 39 percent believe it is morally acceptable. In the same poll, 50 percent of Americans said they believe abortions should be legal under certain circumstances, versus legal under any circumstances (27 percent) or illegal in all circumstances (22 percent).[8]

In a June 2011 Gallup Poll, 62 percent of respondents said they think abortion should be legal in the first trimester of pregnancy, while 24 percent and 10 percent of respondents thought abortion should be legal in the second and third trimesters, respectively.[9]

Social and Political Atmospheres

Courts and politicians reflect the nation as a whole. In a reaction to the wave of social rights and feminism that led to the *Roe v. Wade* decision, more recently, conservative values have been gradually shifting the tide away from abortion. In 2009, for the first time since it began polling on abortion in 1973, Gallup found that more people identified themselves as pro-life than as pro-choice.[7] That trend reversed in 2010 and 2011, although the number of people who considered themselves

133

Abortion has been a challenging issue for hundreds of years.
That fact is unlikely to change.

conservative in 2010 remained steady at 40 percent, with 21 percent of Americans saying they were liberal, and 34 percent indicating they were moderate.[10]

Even with this conservative trend, polls consistently show that most Americans want *Roe v. Wade* to remain intact, though they may not be aware of what that means. Some people are perhaps confused about the abortion ruling. Many people favor keeping *Roe v. Wade*, yet they also favor some legal restrictions that would not be allowed by *Roe*. A 2008 Gallup poll showed 52 percent of respondents wanted *Roe v. Wade* to remain intact, while 33 percent wanted it overturned. Fifteen percent of respondents were undecided.[11] In a 2010 Washington Post–ABC News poll, 60 percent of respondents said they did not want *Roe v. Wade* overturned, while 38 percent said they were in favor of it being overturned.[12] And in 2011, Gallup found that Americans polled supported five of the seven restrictions presented, including parental consent for women under the age of 18 and a waiting period of 24 hours. The two restrictions opposed by a majority of respondents were prohibition of federal funding to clinics providing abortions and a law that would allow health-care providers and pharmacists to not provide abortion drugs or procedures.[13]

If *Roe* Is Overturned

If *Roe v. Wade* is overturned, unless the federal government quickly passes a national abortion law, state laws will prevail. At least 20 states have laws that could be used to restrict or ban abortions, including statutes that were in effect before the 1973 *Roe* decision and never taken off the books. Seven states have laws that protect the woman's right to choose abortion before viability or when needed to protect the woman's life or health.

Even if illegal, it is doubtful women will stop seeking abortions. History tells us that when faced with an unwanted pregnancy, some women will choose to terminate their pregnancies regardless of whether the procedure is legal. In states where abortion is illegal, it is likely that women will travel to a state where it is legal. Poor women without the means to travel may turn to underground illegal abortions, as they did before *Roe v. Wade*. Under some fetal-protection laws, doctors can potentially be charged with murdering the fetus—with penalties of life in prison or death—so it is uncertain how many doctors will be willing to perform illegal abortions in states with these laws. If medication abortions are deemed illegal along with surgical procedures, a black market in these drugs and their administration may emerge.

If the Supreme Court does not overturn *Roe*, federal legislation banning abortion is the other way pro-life policy may become law. Given the ambivalent feelings Americans have toward the issue, passing this kind of legislation is unlikely. If it does, Joseph W. Dellapenna, a law professor at Villanova University, noted of the approximately 30 million women who have had abortions since 1973,

> *If a significant minority of those women are willing to become active resisters of restrictive abortion laws, the enforcement of such laws will be seriously weakened and might fail altogether.*[14]

MCCORVEY: CATHOLIC AND PRO-LIFE

In the years since the landmark *Roe v. Wade* case, McCorvey had a change of heart and became a member of the pro-life movement and a Catholic. She has stated that she believes Weddington and Coffee used her as a pawn when selecting her as their plaintiff, Jane Roe. McCorvey is a pro-life speaker and activist. In 2009, she was arrested for unlawful conduct while demonstrating at the Senate confirmation hearing for Supreme Court Justice Sonia Sotomayor.

Pregnancy changes a woman's life.

Finding Compromise

Supreme Court rulings usually put an issue to rest,
but abortion is as controversial today as it was in 1973.
N. E. H. Hull and Peter Charles Hoffer, professors of
law and history, respectively, examined the abortion
controversy in US history. They noted of the
landmark case,

The storm that formed during and after Roe was so bitter because both sides saw abortion not as a simple, limited legal issue but one that represented two opposing moral worlds.[15]

With *Roe v. Wade*, the pro-choice moral world of autonomous women in charge of their lives and their bodies collided with the pro-life view that connects protection of the unborn with faith and beliefs about the right to life and the sanctity of life. In an ideal world, every pregnancy is planned and there is no need for abortion. But the world is far from ideal. Still, a generation of women has grown to adulthood with access—however limited—to legal abortions. For now, at least, *Roe v. Wade* continues to be the law of the land. Regardless of what the future brings, the fact remains that *Roe v. Wade* is a landmark Supreme Court case. What is also clear is that no ruling will cement a single belief in Americans' minds. It also will not change the fact women will still seek abortions and that the decision to have an abortion is life changing for any woman. ∼

TIMELINE OF EVENTS AND RULINGS

1873	**March**	Congress passes the Comstock Act, criminalizing abortion and birth control.
1916	**October**	Family planning crusader Margaret Sanger opens the first birth control clinic in the United States.
1965	**June**	In *Griswold v. Connecticut*, the Supreme Court rules a law against contraceptives violates a right of marital privacy.
1970	**February**	McCorvey meets with Sarah Weddington and Linda Coffee.
	March 3	Coffee files the case *Roe v. Wade* at the federal courthouse in Dallas, Texas.
	May 22	*Roe v. Wade* arguments begin.
	June 17	A three-judge panel rules in favor of Roe.
1971	**May 3**	The Supreme Court announces it will hear *Roe* with a Georgia abortion case, *Doe v. Bolton*.
	December 13	The Supreme Court hears oral arguments for *Roe v. Wade*.
1972	**June 26**	The Supreme Court sends notice that *Roe v. Wade* is scheduled for reargument.
	October 11	*Roe v. Wade* is reargued before the Supreme Court.

1973	**January 22**	The Supreme Court upholds the lower court's ruling on *Roe v. Wade*.
1989	**July 3**	*Webster v. Reproductive Health Services* becomes the first major Supreme Court challenge to *Roe*.
1992	**June 29**	The court upholds *Roe* in *Planned Parenthood v. Casey* but gives states more leeway in deciding fetal viability and to restrict access to abortion.
1993	**March 10**	David Gunn becomes the first doctor murdered for performing abortions.
1994	**May 26**	The Freedom of Access to Clinic Entrances Act becomes a law.
2000	**June 28**	The court rules in *Stenberg v. Carhart* that Nebraska's partial-birth abortion ban is too vague.
2003	**November 5**	The Partial-Birth Abortion Ban Act becomes law.
2004	**April 1**	The Unborn Victims of Violence Act becomes law.
2007	**April**	In April, the Supreme Court upholds the federal ban on partial-birth abortions.
2009	**January**	Barack Obama restores aid to embryonic stem-cell research, abortion on military bases, and overseas abortion counseling.

GLOSSARY

birth control
>A method, device, or medication that prevents pregnancy.

common law
>A body or system of law based on reason and general custom; applied to situations not covered by legislation.

conception
>The process of becoming pregnant involving fertilization.

conjecture
>Opinion or judgment based on little or no evidence.

conservative
>Traditional; likely to have existing or long-held views.

dissolute
>Lacking restraint, being indulgent.

divisive
>Tending to cause division or disagreement.

euthanasia
>Killing a person suffering from a painful and incurable disease or in an irreversible coma in a relatively painless manner; mercy killing.

flapper
>A young woman of the 1920s who went against social norms often by cutting her hair short and wearing short dresses.

liberal

Broad-minded; not strict; not held to traditional beliefs.

panacea

Something that fixes everything; a cure-all.

partial-birth abortion

An abortion usually performed in the late second or third trimester, in which the fetus is allowed to pass into the birth canal, at which point death is induced.

rubella

Also called German measles, a contagious viral disease that can cause birth defects if contracted early in pregnancy.

therapeutic abortion

The termination of a pregnancy to prevent harm to the pregnant woman.

trimester

One of the three periods of equal length—approximately three months—into which human pregnancy is divided.

viability

The capability to live.

BRIEFS

Petitioner

Jane Roe, the pseudonym for Norma McCorvey

Respondent

Henry Wade, district attorney, Dallas County, Texas

Date of Ruling

January 22, 1973

Summary of Impacts

Abortion has been a controversial issue in US history. State statutes against abortion began appearing in the nineteenth and early twentieth centuries, reflecting concerns over a proliferation of abortion. Most state abortion statutes remained in effect through the late 1960s, when a combination of the women's movement, a liberal social atmosphere, and the perceived health and emotional risks of illegal abortions resulted in a wave of legislation and lawsuits challenging the constitutionality of state abortion laws banning the procedure. One such case, *Roe v. Wade*, was heard in Dallas, Texas, by a three-judge panel on May 22, 1970. The panel ruled in favor of Roe but not all plaintiffs named in the case. *Roe* was appealed directly to the Supreme Court, where it was first heard on December 13, 1971. The case was reargued on October 11, 1972. On January 22, 1973, the Supreme Court upheld the lower court's decision in a 7–2 ruling, deeming that a right to privacy under the due process clause of the Constitution's

Fourteenth Amendment extended to a woman's choice to have an abortion.

Roe v. Wade made irrelevant most state abortion statutes but allowed states to regulate abortion somewhat in the second and third trimesters of pregnancy. Since 1973, Roe v. Wade has been repeatedly challenged in court. It was upheld, but weakened, in Planned Parenthood of Southeastern Pennsylvania v. Casey (1992). Given more leeway to decide fetal viability after this decision, states began passing more restrictive abortion legislation. Roe v. Wade pitted pro-life forces against pro-choice forces, who continue to disagree over the rights of the unborn fetus versus the woman's right to control her body. The case has continued to affect politics, Supreme Court nominations, and a number of related life issues, including stem-cell research and euthanasia.

Quote

"We forthwith acknowledge our awareness of the sensitive and emotional nature of the abortion controversy, of the vigorous opposing views, even among physicians, and of the deep and seemingly absolute convictions that the subject inspires. One's philosophy, one's experiences, one's exposure to the raw edges of human experience, one's religious training, one's attitudes toward life and family and their values, and the moral standards one establishes and seeks to observe, are all likely to influence and to color one's thinking and conclusions about abortion."

—Justice Harry Blackmun, delivering the majority opinion,

Roe v. Wade, January 22, 1973

ADDITIONAL RESOURCES

Selected Bibliography

Dellapenna, Joseph W. *Dispelling the Myths of Abortion History.* Durham, NC: Carolina Academic Press, 2006. Print.

Faux, Marian. Roe v. Wade: *The Untold Story of the Landmark Supreme Court Decision that Made Abortion Legal.* 2nd ed. New York: Macmillan, 2001. Print.

Hull, N. E. H., and Peter Charles Hoffer. Roe v. Wade*: The Abortion Rights Controversy in American History.* 2nd ed. Lawrence: UP of Kansas, 2010. Print.

McCorvey, Norma, and Andy Meisler. *I Am Roe: My Life,* Roe v. Wade*, and Freedom of Choice.* New York: Harper, 1994. Print.

Weddington, Sarah. *A Question of Choice.* New York: Penguin, 1993. Print.

Further Readings

Alcorn, Randy. *ProLife Answers to ProChoice Arguments.* Sisters, OR: Multnomah, 2000. Print.

Gold, Susan Dudley. Roe v. Wade*: A Woman's Choice?* Tarrytown: Benchmark, 2005. Print.

Hillstrom, Laurie Collier. Roe v. Wade. Detroit, MI: Omnigraphics, 2008. Print.

Web Links

To learn more about *Roe v. Wade*, visit ABDO Publishing Company online at **www.abdopublishing.com**. Web sites about *Roe* are featured on our Book Links page. These links are routinely monitored and updated to provide the most current information available.

Places to Visit

Earle Cabell Federal Building and Courthouse

1100 Commerce Street, Room 1452, Dallas, TX 75242
214-753-2200
www.txnd.uscourts.gov/index.html
Roe v. Wade was launched here when papers in the case were filed. Tours are scheduled upon request.

National Archives Experience

Constitution Avenue NW, Washington, DC 20408
www.archives.gov/nae/
866-272-6272, 877-444-6777 (reservations)
Tour the public vaults and view the US Constitution.

US Supreme Court

One First Street NE, Washington, DC 20543
202-479-3000
www.supremecourt.gov/visiting/visiting.aspx
Visitors are encouraged to explore the building. Educational programs include lectures, exhibits, and a film specifically for visitors.

SOURCE NOTES

Chapter 1. Looking for Help

1. Sarah Weddington. *A Question of Choice.* New York: Putnam, 1992. Print. 34.

2. Norma McCorvey and Andy Meisler. *I Am Roe: My Life,* Roe v. Wade, *and Freedom of Choice.* New York: HarperCollins, 1994. Print. 122.

3. Ibid.

4. Ibid. 115.

Chapter 2. About Abortion

1. Marian Faux. *Roe v. Wade: The Untold Story of the Landmark Supreme Court Decision that Made Abortion Legal.* 2nd ed. New York: Macmillan, 2000. Print. 55.

2. George H. Napheys. *The Physical Life of Woman: Advice to the Maiden, Wife, and Mother.* London, 1893. 93. *Google Book Search.* Web. 20 Feb. 2012.

3. George H. Napheys. *The Physical Life of Woman: Advice to the Maiden, Wife, and Mother.* London, 1893. 99. *Google Book Search.* Web. 20 Feb. 2012.

4. Ibid.

5. Ibid.

6. Alice B. Stockham. *Tokology: A Book for Every Woman.* Chicago, 1897. 250. *Google Book Search.* Web. 20 Feb. 2012.

Chapter 3. The United States, 1900–1970

1. Elizabeth Cady Stanton. "Child Murder," *The Revolution,* 12 Mar. 1868. *Feminine and Nonviolence Studies.* Web. 6 Feb. 2012.

2. Ibid.

3. N. E. H. Hull and Peter Charles Hoffer. Roe v. Wade*: The Abortion Rights Controversy in American History.* Lawrence: UP of Kansas, 2001. Print. 27.

4. Leslie J. Reagan. *When Abortion Was a Crime: Women, Medicine, and Law in the United States,* 1867–1973. London: U of California P, 1997. Print. 23.

5. Ibid.

6. N. E. H. Hull and Peter Charles Hoffer. Roe v. Wade*: The Abortion Rights Controversy in American History.* 2nd ed. Lawrence: UP of Kansas, 2001. Print. 65.

7. Ibid.

8. Joseph W. Dellapenna. *Dispelling the Myths of Abortion History.* Durham, NC: Carolina Academic Press, 2006. Print. 488–489.

9. N. E. H. Hull and Peter Charles Hoffer. Roe v. Wade*: The Abortion Rights Controversy in American History.* 2nd ed. Lawrence: UP of Kansas, 2001. Print. 92.

10. Edward M. Wise. "Abortion." *Encyclopedia of Crime and Justice.* 2002. *Encyclopedia.com.* HighBeam Research, 2012. Web. 20 Feb. 2012.

Chapter 4. Two Young Attorneys, One Historical Moment

1. Sarah Weddington. *A Question of Choice.* New York: Putnam, 1992. Print. 37.

2. Ibid. 19.

3. Donald P. Kommers, John E. Finn, and Gary J. Jacobsohn. *American Constitutional Law: Essays, Cases, and Comparative Notes.* 3rd ed. Lanham, MD: Rowman & Littlefield, 2010. 11. *Google Book Search.* Web. 20 Feb. 2012.

4. Sarah Weddington. *A Question of Choice.* New York: Putnam, 1992. Print. 15.

5. Griswold v. Connecticut. 381 US 479. Supreme Court of the US. 1965. *Supreme Court Collection.* Legal Information Inst., Cornell U Law School, n.d. Web. 20 Feb. 2012.

6. Sarah Weddington. *A Question of Choice.* New York: Putnam, 1992. Print. 49.

7. Joseph W. Dellapenna. *Dispelling the Myths of Abortion History.* Durham, NC: Carolina Academic Press, 2006. Print. 551–554.

8. Sarah Weddington. *A Question of Choice.* New York: Putnam, 1992. Print. 54.

Chapter 5. Constructing and Filing *Roe v. Wade*

1. Sarah Weddington. *A Question of Choice.* New York: Putnam, 1992. Print. 54.

2. Ibid. 55–56.

3. Ibid. 52.

4. Ibid. 52–53.

5. Ibid. 62.

SOURCE NOTES CONTINUED

6. "Bill of Rights Transcript." *The Charters of Freedom.* US National Archives and Records Administration, n.d. Web. 20 Feb. 2012.

Chapter 6. The Dallas Hearing

1. Sarah Weddington. *A Question of Choice.* New York: Putnam, 1992. Print. 63.

2. Ibid. 64.

3. N. E. H. Hull and Peter Charles Hoffer. Roe v. Wade*: The Abortion Rights Controversy in American History.* 2nd ed. Lawrence: UP of Kansas, 2001. Print. 123.

4. "Bill of Rights Transcript." *The Charters of Freedom.* US National Archives and Records Administration, n.d. Web. 20 Feb. 2012.

5. Sarah Weddington. *A Question of Choice.* New York: Putnam, 1992. Print. 66.

6. Ian Shapiro. *Abortion: The Supreme Court Decisions, 1965–2000.* 2nd ed. Indianapolis: Hacket, 2001. 23. *Google Book Search.* Web. 20 Feb. 2012.

7. Roy M. Mersky and Gary R. Hartman. *A Documentary History of the Legal Aspects of Abortion in the United States:* Roe v. Wade. Vol. 2. Buffalo: Hein. 1993. 1221. *Google Book Search.* Web. 20 Feb. 2012

8. Norma McCorvey and Andy Meisler. *I Am Roe: My Life,* Roe v. Wade*, and Freedom of Choice.* New York: HarperCollins, 1994. Print. 127.

9. Alex Witchel. "At Home With: Norma McCorvey; of Roe, Dreams and Choices." 28 July 1994. *New York Times.* New York Times Company, 2012. Web. 12 Mar. 2012.

Chapter 7. *Roe* Goes to the Supreme Court

1. Marian Faux. Roe v. Wade: *The Untold Story of the Landmark Supreme Court Decision that Made Abortion Legal.* New York: Macmillan, 1988. 257. Print.

2. "History." *Americans United for Life.* Americans United for Life, n.d. Web. 12 Feb. 2012.

3. Sarah Weddington. *A Question of Choice.* New York: Putnam, 1992. Print. 99.

4. Ian Shapiro. *Abortion: The Supreme Court Decisions, 1965–2000.* 2nd ed. Indianapolis: Hacket, 2001. 23. *Google Book Search.* Web. 20 Feb. 2012.

5. Sarah Weddington. *A Question of Choice.* New York: Putnam, 1992. Print. 82.

6. Roe v. Wade. 410 US 113. Supreme Court of the US, 1973. *Oyez US Supreme Court Media.* IIT Chicago-Kent College of Law, 2011. Web. 20 Feb. 2012.

7. Marian Faux. Roe v. Wade: *The Untold Story of the Landmark Supreme Court Decision that Made Abortion Legal.* New York: Macmillan, 1988. Print. 259.

8. Roe v. Wade. 410 US 113. Supreme Court of the US, 1973. *Oyez US Supreme Court Media*, IIT Chicago-Kent College of Law, 2011. Web. 20 Feb. 2012.

9. Ibid.

10. Ibid.

11. Ibid.

12. Ibid.

13. Ibid.

14. Ibid.

Chapter 8. Reargument and a Decision

1. Sarah Weddington. *A Question of Choice.* New York: Putnam, 1992. Print. 131.

2. N. E. H. Hull and Peter Charles Hoffer. Roe v. Wade: *The Abortion Rights Controversy in American History.* 2nd ed. Lawrence: UP of Kansas, 2001. Print. 170.

3. Sarah Weddington. *A Question of Choice.* New York: Putnam, 1992. Print. 140.

4. Ibid. 151.

5. Roe v. Wade. 410 US 113. Supreme Court of the US, 1973. *Oyez US Supreme Court Media*, IIT Chicago-Kent College of Law, 2011. Web. 20 Feb. 2012.

6. Ibid.

7. Ibid.

8. Ibid.

9. Ibid.

10. Sarah Weddington. *A Question of Choice*. New York: Putnam, 1992. Print. 165.

11. Ibid.

12. Ibid.

13. Ibid. 166.

14. Ibid.

15. Roe v. Wade. 410 US 113. Supreme Court of the US. 1973. *FindLaw: Cases and Codes*. FindLaw, 2012. Web. 20 Feb. 2012.

16. Norma McCorvey and Andy Meisler. *I Am Roe: My Life,* Roe v. Wade, *and Freedom of Choice*. New York: HarperCollins, 1994. Print. 150.

Chapter 9. Early Challenges to *Roe*

1. Lilo T. Strauss, Joy Herndon, Jeani Chang, Wilda Y. Parker, Sonya V. Bowens, and Cynthia J. Berg. "Abortion Surveillance—United States, 2002." *MMWR*. Centers for Disease Control and Prevention, 15 Nov. 2005. Web. 12 Mar. 2012

2. Joseph W. Dellapenna. *Dispelling the Myths of Abortion History*. Durham, NC: Carolina Academic Press, 2006. Print. 554–557.

3. Marian Faux. Roe v. Wade: *The Untold Story of the Landmark Supreme Court Decision that Made Abortion Legal*. New York: Macmillan, 1988. Print. 305.

4. "Abortion." *Catholic Answers*. Catholic Answers, 10 Aug. 2004. Web. 19 Mar. 2012.

5. "Abortion 2010." *National Association of Evangelicals*. National Association of Evangelicals, 2009. Web. 20 Feb. 2012.

6. Ed Magnuson and Patricia Delaney. "Explosions Over Abortion." *Time*. Time, 14 Jan. 1985. Web. 20 Feb. 2012.

7. Ibid.

8. N. E. H. Hull and Peter Charles Hoffer. Roe v. Wade: *The Abortion Rights Controversy in American History*. 2nd ed. Lawrence: UP of Kansas, 2001. Print. 213–214.

9. Marian Faux. Roe v. Wade: *The Untold Story of the Landmark Supreme Court Decision that Made Abortion Legal*. New York: Macmillan, 1988. Print. 315.

10. N. E. H. Hull and Peter Charles Hoffer. Roe v. Wade: *The Abortion Rights Controversy in American History*. 2nd ed. Lawrence: UP of Kansas, 2001. Print. 215.

11. Planned Parenthood of Southeastern Pa. v. Casey. 505 US 833. Supreme Court Collection. Legal Information Inst., Cornell U Law School, n.d. Web. 20 Feb. 2012.

12. Norma McCorvey and Andy Meisler. *I Am Roe: My Life,* Roe v. Wade, *and Freedom of Choice.* New York: HarperCollins, 1994. Print. 174.

Chapter 10. *Roe*'s Broad Shadow

1. N. E. H. Hull and Peter Charles Hoffer. Roe v. Wade: *The Abortion Rights Controversy in American History.* 2nd ed. Lawrence: UP of Kansas, 2001. Print. 279.

2. "Abortion." *Gallup.* Gallup, 2012. Web. 20 Feb. 2012.

3. Lydia Saad. "*Roe v. Wade* Has Positive Public Image." *Gallup.* Gallup, 20 Jan. 2003. Web. 20 Feb. 2012.

4. N. E. H. Hull and Peter Charles Hoffer. Roe v. Wade: *The Abortion Rights Controversy in American History.* 2nd ed. Lawrence: UP of Kansas, 2001. Print. 280.

5. "Who We Are." *Democrats for Life of America.* Democrats for Life of America, n.d. Web. 19 Mar. 2012.

6. "About Us." *Republican Majority for Choice.* ElectionMall Technologies, 2005. Web. 19 Mar. 2012.

7. Lydia Saad. "Republicans More Unified than Democrats on Abortion." *Gallup.* Gallup, 6 June 2011. Web. 19 Mar. 2012.

8. "Facts on Induced Abortion in the United States." *In Brief.* Guttmacher Institute, May 2011. Web. 20 Feb. 2012.

9. Elizabeth G. Raymond and David A. Grimes. "The Comparative Safety of Legal Induced Abortion and Childbirth in the United States." *Obstetrics & Gynecology.* American College of Obstetricians and Gynecologists, 2012. Web. 5 Feb. 2012.

Chapter 11. Abortion Today and the Future of *Roe*

1. "Births, Deaths, Marriages, and Divorces." *Statistical Abstract of the United States: 2011.* 75. US Centers for Disease Control and Prevention, 2011. Web. 19 Mar. 2012.

2. "Facts on Induced Abortion in the United States." *In Brief.* Guttmacher Institute, May 2011. Web. 20 Feb. 2012.

3. N. E. H. Hull and Peter Charles Hoffer. Roe v. Wade: *The Abortion Rights Controversy in American History*. Lawrence: UP of Kansas, 2001. Print. 78.

4. "The Abortion Pill (Medication Abortion)." *Planned Parenthood*. Planned Parenthood Federation of America, 2012. Web. 20 Feb. 2012.

5. Facts on Induced Abortion in the United States." *In Brief*. Guttmacher Institute, May 2011. Web. 20 Feb. 2012.

6. Wolfgang Saxon. "Henry Wade, Prosecutor in National Spotlight, Dies at 86." *New York Times*. New York Times Company, 2 Mar. 2001. Web. 20 Feb. 2012.

7. "Abortion." *Gallup*. Gallup, 2012. Web. 20 Feb. 2012.

8. Ibid.

9. Lydia Saad. "Common State Abortion Restrictions Spark Mixed Reviews." *Gallup*. Gallup, 25 Jul. 2011. Web. 19 Mar. 2012

10. Lydia Saad. "Conservatives Continue to Outnumber Moderates in 2010." *Gallup*. Gallup, 16 Dec. 2010. Web. 20 Feb. 2012.

11. "Abortion." *Gallup*. Gallup, 2012. Web. 20 Feb. 2012.

12. Steven Ertelt. "Poll: Americans Wanting *Roe* Abortion Ruling Overturned Reaches New High." LifeNews.com. 4 May 2010. Web. 20 Feb. 2012.

13. Lydia Saad. "Common State Abortion Restrictions Spark Mixed Reviews." *Gallup*. Gallup, 25 July 2011. Web. 20 Feb. 2012.

14. Joseph W. Dellapenna. *Dispelling the Myths of Abortion History*. Durham, NC: Carolina Academic Press, 2006. Print. 989.

15. N. E. H. Hull and Peter Charles Hoffer. Roe v. Wade: *The Abortion Rights Controversy in American History*. 2nd ed. Lawrence: UP of Kansas, 2001. Print. 338.

INDEX

About the Author

Melissa Higgins is the author of more than ten books for children and young adults, with topics ranging from addiction and divorce to baseball and biographies. Her stories for young readers have appeared in *Skipping Stones* and *Characters* magazines. Before pursuing a writing career, she worked as a mental health counselor in schools and private practice.

About the Content Consultant

Joseph W. Dellapenna earned a BBA from the University of Michigan, a JD from the Detroit College of Law, and Masters of Laws from George Washington University and Columbia University. He is a professor of law at Villanova University, where he teaches on a variety of law topics.